Better Homes and Gardens®

cut the sugar cookbook

Meredith® Books
Des Moines, Iowa

Better Homes and Gardens®

cut the sugar cookbook

Editor: Stephanie Karpinske, R.D.
Contributing Writer: Jill Melton, R.D.
Contributing Editor: Janet Figg
Graphic Designers: Chad Johnston, Daniel Fish (On-Purpos, Inc.)
Copy Chief: Terri Fredrickson
Publishing Operations Manager: Karen Schirm
Senior Editor, Asset and Information Manager: Phillip Morgan
Editorial and Design Production Coordinator: Mary Lee Gavin
Editorial Assistants: Cheryl Eckert, Kairee Windsor
Book Production Managers: Pam Kvitne, Marjorie J. Schenkelberg, Rick von Holdt, Mark Weaver
Contributing Copy Editor: Amanda Knief
Contributing Proofreaders: Callie Dunbar, Debra Jensen, Susan J. Kling
Indexer: Spectrum Communications, Inc.
Test Kitchen Director: Lynn Blanchard
Test Kitchen Product Supervisor: Marilyn Cornelius
Test Kitchen Home Economists: Juliana Hale; Laura Harms, R.D.; Jennifer Kalinowski, R.D.; Maryellyn Krantz; Jill Moberly; Dianna Nolin; Colleen Weeden; Lori Wilson; Charles Worthington

MEREDITH® BOOKS
Executive Director, Editorial: Gregory H. Kayko
Executive Director, Design: Matt Strelecki
Senior Editor/Group Manager: Jan Miller
Senior Associate Design Director: Doug Samuelson
Marketing Product Manager: Gina Rickert

Publisher and Editor In Chief: James D. Blume
Executive Editor: Linda Raglan Cunningham
Executive Director, New Business Development: Todd M. Davis
Executive Director, Sales: Ken Zagor
Director, Operations: George A. Susral
Director, Production: Douglas M. Johnston
Director, Marketing: Amy Nichols
Business Director: Jim Leonard

Vice President and General Manager: Douglas J. Guendel

BETTER HOMES AND GARDENS® MAGAZINE
Editor In Chief: Karol DeWulf Nickell
Deputy Editor, Food and Entertaining: Nancy Hopkins

MEREDITH PUBLISHING GROUP
President: Jack Griffin
Executive Vice President: Bob Mate

MEREDITH CORPORATION
Chairman and Chief Executive Officer: William T. Kerr
President and Chief Operating Officer: Stephen M. Lacy

In memoriam: E.T. Meredith III (1933-2003)

Our seal on the back cover assures you that every recipe in *Cut The Sugar* has been tested in the Better Homes and Gardens® Test Kitchen. This means that each recipe is practical and reliable, and meets our high standards of taste appeal. We guarantee your satisfaction with this book for as long as you own it.

contents

the
sweet world
we live in

You can stroll down the aisle of any supermarket and see that sugar has invaded everything. Microwave popcorn is now imbued with sugar in "kettle corn;" there are sugar-coated almonds and peanuts; colored marshmallows are in cereal; and hot fudge sundae is a toaster pastry flavor. Our food supply has been attacked by sugar and candy at every turn.

If you're looking to better understand sugar and how to limit it in your child's diet, you've come to the right place. This book clears up the myths regarding sugar and health and helps you sort through the vast shopping conundrums that lurk in every aisle of the supermarket.

It provides you with an arsenal of nutritious recipes similar to the foods your kids already love. There are Chicken Nuggets that aren't fried, and pizza made with low-sugar tomato sauce and healthful toppings. Desserts such as Oatmeal-Banana Bread Pudding and Fantastic Fruit Kabobs are kid-friendly. But before you get to the recipes, let's take a closer look at our sugary-sweet environment.

But that recipe never had sugar!

Most of the recipes in this book are low-sugar alternatives to foods you normally think of as being high in sugar. But you'll also find some recipes that never had sugar. That's because we wanted to include a variety of healthful recipes that kids would love in order to create a complete cookbook that offers parents solutions for every meal. So along with low-sugar desserts and snacks, we also have included low-fat, nutrient-rich salads, soups, pizzas, and sandwiches. These foods are easy-to-make, fast alternatives to the highly processed foods that kids may be used to eating.

THE EVOLUTION OF THE SWEET TOOTH Humans love sugar. As infants, we pucker when we're given sugar water and scowl when given something bitter. Research has shown that babies have an unlearned preference for sweet and salty tastes and the rejection of sour and bitter tastes. In prehistoric times, this was a good thing as most poisonous foods were bitter and most sweet foods (including mother's milk) were safe. Though we don't rely on it for safety anymore, that inborn preference for sweets stayed with us, making sugary treats hard to resist.

SUGAR OVERLOAD Most people agree that our kids eat too much sugar. According to the United States Department of Agriculture (USDA), people consuming 2,000 calories a day should eat no more than about 10 teaspoons (40 grams) of added sugar (about the amount in a can of soda). USDA surveys show that the average American is consuming about 40 teaspoons of sugar per day.

Sugar now accounts for 16 percent of the calories consumed by the average American and 20 percent of a teenager's calories. Compare that to 1978, when added sugars provided only 11 percent of the average person's calories.

Do we really need to worry about all those extra sugar grams? Sugar gets the blame for lots of problems—from cavities to hyperactivity—so here's the scoop on what to worry (and not worry) about when it comes to sugar.

did you know?

From 1985 to the present, sugar consumption has risen by 2% each year.

CALORIES WE CAN'T AFFORD In 2002, 16 percent of kids ages 6–19 were overweight, triple what it was in 1980. And 8 out of 10 Americans over 25 are overweight. This has led to a 76 percent increase in type 2 diabetes in adults 30-40 years old since 1990. The World Health Organization reported in 2000 that the number of obese adults was 300 million worldwide.

The rise of obesity can't be blamed on any one thing. Dwindling activity levels are one of the biggest reasons for spiraling weights. But sugar- and fat-filled foods in increasingly large portions aren't helping. Go to most any movie theatre in the United States and you'll find the large drink (a whopping 44 ounces) costs only 25 cents more than the medium size (a "petite" 32 ounces).

The problem is that most people, even growing kids, can't afford these excess calories. The less active we are, the less we can eat. The food we do eat needs to be full of vitamins, minerals, and other nutrients in order to meet our needs. Most high sugar (and high fat) foods give us calories but not much else. These foods taste good, so we eat lots of them and all those excess calories end up as fat. By the end of the day, we haven't met our body's nutritional needs and we're packing on the pounds. So although added sugars can't be solely to blame for obesity, it's clearly a contributor to the problem.

TOOTH DECAY If there's one thing we do know about sugar, it's the dentist's nemesis (or best friend, depending on how you view it). Sugar, saliva, and bacteria create a formidable combination that can lead to tooth decay. Minutes after eating sugar (particularly sucrose), glycoproteins stick to the teeth to start the formation of plaque. Sticky candy is the worst offender, but all sweet foods have the potential for tooth decay. A diet rich in calcium and fluoride leads to stronger teeth—another good reason to substitute milk for soda.

DIABETES In the past, sugar was blamed for causing diabetes. But sugar, in and of itself, does not cause diabetes. It can be caused by genetics, ethnicity, and, in many cases, obesity.

Soda Nation

Soft drinks, which contain about 10 teaspoons of sugar per 12-ounce can, are one of the main sources of sugar in our diet. Per person, we guzzle down twice as many sodas as we did in 1974. In addition to weight gain, sugar may contribute to osteoporosis because many kids, especially teenage girls, drink soda instead of calcium-rich milk. Twenty years ago, teens drank almost twice as much milk as soda; today they consume almost twice as much soda as milk.

did you know?

The average fast-food soft drink in the 1950s was 8 ounces; today the size given out with a kid's meal is 12 ounces.

Simply defined, diabetes is a condition that affects the way the body uses energy from sugar. There are two types of diabetes. Type 1 diabetes is usually diagnosed in children and occurs when the body doesn't produce enough insulin. Type 2, the most common, is usually diagnosed in adults, and occurs when the body doesn't produce enough insulin or the cells ignore it. Being overweight increases the risk for type 2 diabetes; the theory is that as cells expand (with increasing weight), they become less receptive to insulin.

As our nation becomes heavier, diabetes rates are going up. Between 1997 and 2002, there was a 27 percent increase in diabetes. Eighty percent of type 2 diabetes is related to obesity, and it may be right around the corner for many of our children. A new study shows that one in four overweight children is showing early signs of type 2 diabetes.

Watching sugar intake for a diabetic is important, but really all carbohydrates need to be monitored since they all turn into glucose (a simple sugar) in the body. Today's diabetic is able to have a little sugar as long as it's considered in their total allowance of carbohydrates for the day.

HYPERACTIVITY We've all heard it before: "The kids are bouncing off the walls because they've had too much sugar." This is a popular myth, one which parents like to use to justify or explain less than angelic behavior. But research has not confirmed any connection between sugar and hyperactivity. Nor has research found any correlation between artificial sweeteners, flavors, or colors and hyperactivity.

MORE SUGAR, PLEASE! A spoonful of sugar helps the medicine go down—and apparently everything else. Sugar is in everything from catsup to canned soup to salad dressing. While these products aren't supplying the majority of the sugar in our diets, they're still contributing to the "sweetening of our taste buds." The more sugar we get used to, the more we want.

Try this simple experiment. Eat a grape. Now, eat a cookie, then a grape. On its own, the grape tastes sweet and juicy. After the cookie however, the grape tastes almost sour. So you can see how eventually we need more and more sugar to make things taste sweet.

did you know?
Soft drinks are the best-selling product in the grocery store.

did you know?
The percentage of children who are overweight has tripled since 1970.

You can help break this craving for sweet tastes by relying on natural, fresh ingredients. Processed foods are often full of sugar, even foods that don't really taste sweet, such as catsup and spaghetti sauce. Manufacturers may use sugar as a stabilizer or preservative to keep the product fresh, but in the end it contributes to a sweetness you may not even realize unless you compared it to a homemade equivalent.

So, while it's best to cut back on foods that are obviously high in sugar—baked goods, cereals, yogurts, puddings, soft drinks, juices, candy, and cookies—it's wise to eat less of all processed foods. We need to teach our kids to appreciate foods for their natural flavors, instead of the sugar, salt, and artificial flavors that are packed into most processed items.

SUGAR SENSE Is honey really better than sugar? Is it more nutritious? What about the so-called "raw sugar" we find in brown packets at the local diner? Much that we read would have us believe that so-called "natural" sweeteners, such as honey and maple syrup, are more nutritious than sugar. From a calorie perspective, they're approximately the same as sugar, but recent research does show that honey may have some antioxidant activity. It also contributes flavor as well as sweetness—which is why we've used it in many of these recipes. The "natural raw cane sugar" that is found in the brown packets at restaurants, however, is nutritionally identical to the white stuff; it may just have a bit more flavor from some residual molasses. Like sugar, these sweeteners are pure carbohydrate and contain no fat. Like sugar, the vitamin and mineral content is negligible (molasses does have some potassium and iron, unlike the other sweeteners). Here's how they measure up (see *Sugar's Many Forms* chart at left).

SUGAR'S MANY FORMS

1 TABLESPOON	CALORIES	FAT	CARBOHYDRATES
Brown sugar	52	0	13
Corn syrup	60	0	16
Honey	64	0	17
Maple syrup	52	0	13
Molasses	59	0	15
Pancake syrup	46	0	12
Sugar	48	0	12
Turbinado sugar	46	0	12

Source: ESHA Food Processor Program

THE NAME GAME If you start reading labels, you'll be surprised to find how vast the world of sugars is. Although there are many forms of sugar used in food processing today, one simple rule to know is that anything ending in "ose" is a form of sugar—dextrose, glucose, fructose, maltose, galactose, sucrose.

If you pick up most any bottle of chocolate syrup, you'll find a daunting number of sweeteners in the ingredient list including: high fructose corn syrup, corn syrup, and sugar. Detecting all the sugar in a food product can be difficult as it has many forms, but one is really no better than another. Here are all the forms of sugar you can encounter on a food label:

Cane sugar	High fructose corn	Maple syrup
Corn sweeteners	syrup	Molasses
Corn syrup	Honey	Raw sugar
Dextrin	Invert sugar	Sucrose
Dextrose	Malt	Sucrose syrup
Fruit juice concentrate	Maltose	Turbinado sugar
Glucose-fructose syrup	Malt syrup	

Some of the sugars listed on the Nutrition Facts label are naturally occurring and some added. But added sugars are not chemically different than naturally occurring sugars. To your body, the sugar in fruit is no different than the sugar in a can of soda—although the fruit comes packaged with fiber, vitamins, and minerals and the soda is just sugar and water. In general, the more added sugars a product has, the fewer nutrients it has.

To determine the number of teaspoons of sugar in a food, look at the grams of sugar on the Nutrition Facts label. Divide the grams of sugar by 4 and that's how many teaspoons of sugar the product has. Keep in mind that the USDA recommends no more than 10 teaspoons of added sugar per day.

In addition to the Nutrition Facts label, you may also find sugar levels mentioned on the front of the label for foods that have less sugar. These label claims are defined as follows:

Reduced sugar means that the product contains 25 percent less sugar than its original counterpart.

Sugar-free foods have less than 0.5 gram of sugar per serving. However, sugar-free does not mean carbohydrate-free. Compare the total carbohydrate content of a sugar-free food with that of the standard product.

No-sugar-added foods do not have any form of sugar added during processing or packaging. However they can still contain natural sugars.

Low-calorie foods have 40 calories or less per serving.

TRICKS OF THE TRADE Despite the assurances of these terms, food labeling can still be tricky. Food manufacturers can be very crafty about making their food appear healthy. In general, be wary of products that tout a "healthy" ingredient.

did you know?

Daily reference values have not been set for sugar because no recommendations have been made for the total amount to eat in a day.

For instance, yogurt-covered raisins sound healthier than chocolate-covered raisins, but in fact, contain more fat and lots of sugar. The yogurt coating is a far cry from the real thing. The ingredient list goes something like this: sugar, partially hydrogenated palm kernel oil, nonfat milk, nonfat yogurt powder, whey—and well, you get the picture.

The individual pudding cups in convenient kids' sizes tout how they're made with real milk. But upon scrutiny of the nutrition label, you'll find they only provide 4 percent of the daily value for calcium—not much. You would have to eat 25 servings to get your calcium quota, which would amount to 2,250 calories and 400 grams of sugar. Many cereal breakfast bars amount to not much more than glorified candy bars. But with terms such as "natural" emblazoned on their boxes, we're led to believe they're a nutritious start to the day.

SWEET NOTHINGS Sugar-free or "diet" foods are not just for dieters; three times as many people relied on diet products in 2004 as they did in 1984. The growth of these products is mainly because of the wide variety of artificial sweeteners available. Today, it's hard to keep track of all the artificial sweeteners—at last count there were 15 currently in use, with six waiting for Food and Drug Administration (FDA) approval.

Overall, the amount of artificial sweeteners we actually consume is relatively small. According to the USDA, it's less than 2 ounces per person per year (compared to nearly 150 pounds of sugar per person per year). That's because artificial sweeteners are intensely sweet, requiring very small amounts. Don't be surprised to find multiple sweeteners on most foods; this is because most of them work synergistically to create more shelf-stable foods.

But are artificial sweeteners and foods made with them okay for kids to eat? Yes, they are, but they shouldn't take up a large part of a child's diet. The occasional diet soft drink or "light product" is fine, and can help to curb calories, but a reliance on these items is not good. As discussed earlier, the more sweetened foods your kids eat, the more sweetness they'll crave and the less they'll want foods that aren't sweet, such as vegetables and even meats. Kids should eat a balanced diet of natural, wholesome foods—lots of fruits and veggies, whole grains, meats, fish, chicken, and milk.

Since artificial sweeteners have flooded the supermarket shelf, here is a quick primer on them.

did you know?
Many fruit-flavored yogurts are full of sugar—some even more than 30 grams per container! Check the label next time you're at the store.

SUCRALOSE (aka Splenda) Approved in April 1998, sucralose is 600 times sweeter than sugar. Sucralose is the new darling sugar substitute because it's viewed as the most natural. That's because it's the only noncaloric sweetener actually made from sugar. It's incredibly stable, which makes it a great ingredient in virtually every type of food and drink. Plus you can bake with it—something not possible with most other sugar substitutes.

Sucralose is beneficial for individuals with diabetes because research demonstrates that sucralose has no effect on carbohydrate metabolism, short- or long-term blood glucose control, or insulin secretion. You can find Splenda in your local supermarket—in packets ready to pour in coffee and tea, and in larger bags for cooking.

SUGAR ALCOHOLS OR POLYOLS Polyols are sugar-free sweeteners and are used cup-for-cup in the same amount as sugar. The following ones are currently used in foods: erythritol, hydrogenated starch hydrolysates, sorbitol, xylitol, mannitol, malitol, lacitol, isomalt.

STEVIA (aka Sweet Leaf) Here is a sweetener that's created a bit of a buzz because it's all natural. Stevia is an extract from a shrub that grows in South America. Our bodies can't metabolize it. Currently Stevia is approved as a supplement but not a food, meaning you can find it in a pharmacy but not a grocery store. Industry experts expect the FDA to approve it in the near future.

ASPARTAME (aka Equal, NutraSweet, and Nutrataste) This is what's found in the little blue packets that adorn restaurant tables everywhere and in the average diet soft drink. It became the sweetener of choice when saccharin fell from grace. It is a derivative of the amino acids aspartic acid and phenylalanine. People with a rare genetic disorder called PKU (diagnosed at birth) can't metabolize phenylalanine, so must avoid aspartame.

In addition to being low in calories, aspartame tastes very similar to sugar. It is 200 times sweeter than sugar and is used in many foods, from drinks to ice cream to puddings. Aspartame also enhances other flavors, so when combined with other sweeteners, its sweetening power grows exponentially. Aspartame loses sweetness with prolonged exposure to heat. However, a new product called Sugar Lite has just hit the market. It's a blend of aspartame and sugar and can be used in baking.

ACESULFAME POTASSIUM (aka Sweet One, Sunette) This noncaloric sweetener was approved by the FDA in 1988. It is 200 times sweeter than sugar and can be found in ice cream, diet soda, juice, and gum.

TAGATOSE (aka Naturlose) Tagatose is a mirror-image form of sugar that's made from milk sugar and lactose. Tagatose can't be digested, so it passes through the body unabsorbed. It is used in candy, cereals, diet drinks, and ice cream.

SACCHARIN (aka Sweet'n Low) Saccharin, 300 times sweeter than sugar, is the oldest of the approved low-calorie sweeteners and has a controversial history. In 1977, the FDA tried to ban saccharin due to research showing it caused cancer in animals. It remained on the market but with a warning on the label. In 2000, the National Institute of Health removed saccharin from its list of carcinogens and the requirement for the warning label was lifted. Saccharin continues to be controversial, although technically deemed safe.

the reality show:
Common Concerns from Parents

What's a parent to do when kids are faced with sugar at every turn? It's a challenge to survive a trip to the supermarket when the checkout lane is packed with candy and gum. Or when your kids are asking for the latest fruit drinks served up in crazy colors packaged with candy straws.

In this world of sugar-infested foods, how do you feed your kids well, keep them happy, and yourself sane? It's a balancing act for sure. Here are some tips and strategies to help.

BIRTHDAY PARTIES It's amazing how many parties and school functions serve that vexing combination of cake (drenched with gooey icing) with punch or fruit juice. The next time you're sending in birthday goodies, try serving low-sugar cookies and lowfat milk, or granola bars with lowfat milk. Either are better options than cake with icing. And they're easier to serve and eat.

WHEN GRANDPARENTS WANT TO SWEETEN YOUR KIDS Most grandparents feel they have earned the right to spoil their grandkids—and do so with pride. But the biggest opportunity for grandparents is often overlooked. And that is to expose the kids to foods that reflect their heritage—different foods that they would not otherwise be exposed to. Tell your parents not to pander to the kids' tastes, but to serve the foods that are part of their lifestyle. This is an opportunity for kids to learn about their heritage and try new things.

THE SCHOOL LUNCH CHALLENGE Nothing can unnerve even the most organized parent like the empty lunch box at 7:30 a.m. Trying to stay fresh, interesting, and nutritious while packing something the kids will eat is a tall order. Here are some suggestions:

Try wraps. Rolling up ham and cheese in a tortilla is inherently more interesting than a sandwich—plus you don't have the crusts to deal with. You can even vary the cheese and sneak in things like spinach leaves or fruit.

Pack leftovers. Many schools have microwaves that kids can use to heat up their lunches. Or pack items that are good at room temperature, such as our Bacon and Cheese Turnovers (see recipe, page 53) or Grilled Veggie Wraps (see recipe, page 95) without the turkey.

Use thermal lunchboxes. Properly packed, foods that need to stay cold, such as Teriyaki Chicken Noodle Salad (see recipe, page 77) and Smoked Turkey and Tortellini Salad (see recipe, page 78) are good lunchbox candidates.

Bag up mini veggies. Try peeled baby carrots, green sweet pepper strips, jicama sticks, or cucumber slices. All have fun colors and add a crunch to lunch.

Toss in cheese sticks. They're easy to pack, easy to eat. Kids love them.

Try peanut butter and crackers. Instead of peanut butter on bread, pack the crackers and peanut butter separately and let your child assemble them at lunchtime.

Add in bananas and grapes. These fruits are kid favorites, convenient, and in their own containers.

AFTER-SCHOOL SNACKS There are lots of recipes in this book for snacks—some that kids can even make. Make sure you have healthful ingredients on hand so your kids can always find something. Here are some other quick ideas:

Mix up your own hot chocolate. Use cocoa powder or baking chocolate instead of prepared mixes. Then add your own sugar to taste. You'll get more chocolate flavor and some fiber with less sugar.

Try malted chocolate milk. Malted milk powder contains only 30 calories and 3 grams of sugar per tablespoon—an ample amount for an 8-ounce cup.

Choose no-sugar-added applesauce. Original applesauce contains apples, high fructose corn syrup, and has 100 calories per cup. No-sugar-added has just that and is comprised of apples, water, and ascorbic acid (vitamin C), and has only 50 calories per cup.

Try a sport drink. If your kids insist on a fruity drink, give them a sport drink. They usually have 50 calories per cup; juice contains double that, on average 100 calories per cup. Or if they must have juice, try one of the new low-sugar or "light" varieties available. Overall, they have two-thirds fewer calories and sugar than their regular counterparts.

Create your own soda. Mix equal parts club soda and juice for a juice spritzer. Since club soda has no calories, this drink contains a fraction of the calories and sugar of traditional soft drinks, or even juice by itself.

Make homemade frozen pops from juice. The kids will get less sugar and more vitamin C. Pour the juice into plastic frozen dessert/popstick containers and freeze. Kids will love making them.

Cut up fruits and veggies. It may seem simple, but when you cut an apple or other fruits and veggies into manageable slices, kids are more apt to eat them.

sugar
by the numbers

1,401 Number of new candy products introduced in 2002—half of which were chocolate.*

3 Percentage of candy sales from "diet candy."*

99 Percentage of households that purchase candy.*

93 Percentage of children who go trick-or-treating at Halloween.

10 Maximum number of teaspoons (equivalent to 40 grams) of added sugar per day you should eat, according to the USDA.

12 Number of teaspoons of sugar in a chocolate-coated, caramel-topped nougat bar wih peanuts.

10 Teaspoons of sugar in a 12-ounce can of soda.

45 Calories in a tablespoon of sugar.

60 Calories in a tablespoon of honey.

14 Grams of sugar in a serving of chocolate-flavored puffed corn cereal.

1 Gram. The amount of sugar in a serving of round toasted oat cereal.

7 Fat grams in ¼ cup of chocolate-covered raisins.

10 Fat grams in ¼ cup of yogurt-covered raisins.

*from www.candyusa.org

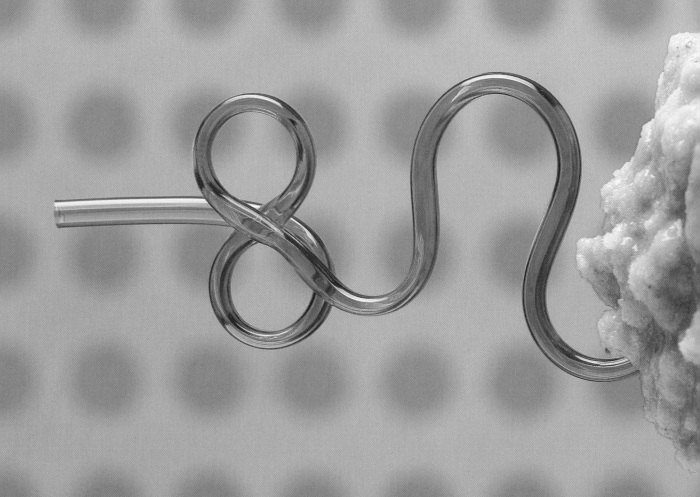

drinks &

munchies

There's no staving off pint-size appetites—when kids get home from school, they're hungry. But forget the chips, soda, and cookies. Give them a fruit smoothie or homemade snack mix, and make that bewitching pre-dinner hour easier to get through.

CRISPY, CRUNCHY SNACK MIX

PREP: 10 minutes **BAKE:** 20 minutes **OVEN:** 300°F **MAKES:** 14 (½-cup) servings

2 cups crispy corn and rice cereal

1½ cups bite-size shredded wheat biscuits

¾ cup peanuts

2 tablespoons butter or margarine

3 tablespoons Dijon-style mustard

1 teaspoon Worcestershire sauce

¼ teaspoon garlic powder

3 cups plain popped popcorn

ONE Place cereal, wheat biscuits, and peanuts in a foil-lined 13X9X2-inch baking pan; set aside. Melt butter in a small saucepan. Remove saucepan from heat; stir in mustard, Worcestershire sauce, and garlic powder until combined. Drizzle over cereal and nut mixture in pan, tossing gently to coat.

TWO Bake mixture, uncovered, in a 300° oven for 20 minutes, gently stirring after 10 minutes. Stir in popcorn. Use foil to remove baked mixture from pan; cool completely. Serve immediately.

Nutrition Facts per serving: 98 cal., 6 g total fat (2 g sat. fat), 5 mg chol., 149 mg sodium, 9 g carbo. (1 g sugar), 1 g fiber, 4 g pro.
Exchanges: ½ Starch, 1 Fat

cut the sugar

This snack mix recipe uses Dijon-style mustard instead of honey mustard, making it lower in sugar. Most Dijon-style mustards are sugar-free.

PEANUT **POPPERS**

START TO FINISH: 10 minutes **MAKES:** 6 ($^2/_3$-cup) servings

4   **cups popped popcorn
    (about 3 tablespoons
    unpopped)**

$^1/_2$ **cup peanuts**

$^1/_3$ **cup dried cranberries
    or raisins**

1   **tablespoon butter**

1   **tablespoon peanut butter**

ONE In a medium bowl stir together popcorn, peanuts, and cranberries. In a small saucepan combine butter and peanut butter. Heat and stir over medium heat until melted. Pour peanut butter mixture over popcorn mixture. Toss to coat. Serve within 6 hours.

Nutrition Facts per serving: 146 cal., 10 g total fat (2 g sat. fat), 5 mg chol., 67 mg sodium, 12 g carbo. (1 g sugar), 2 g fiber, 5 g pro. **Exchanges:** 1 Other Carbo., $^1/_2$ High-Fat Meat, 1 Fat

TACO **MUNCH** MIX

PREP: 5 minutes **BAKE:** 20 minutes **OVEN:** 300°F **MAKES:** 9 (½-cup) servings

- 3 **cups bite-size rice or corn squares cereal**
- 2 **cups small cheese-flavored fish-shaped crackers**
- 2 **cups small pretzels**
- 1 **cup coarsely chopped pecans or sliced almonds**
- ¼ **cup butter or margarine, melted**
- ½ **to 1 teaspoon chili powder**
- ¼ **teaspoon garlic powder**
- 1 **cup dried corn and/or dried sweet peppers**

ONE In a shallow roasting pan combine cereal, crackers, pretzels, and pecans. Set aside.

TWO In a small bowl combine butter, chili powder, and garlic powder. Drizzle butter mixture over cereal mixture; stir gently to coat.

THREE Bake in a 300° oven for 20 minutes or until lightly browned, stirring once or twice. Stir in corn and/or sweet peppers. Spread on a large piece of foil to cool. Store in an airtight container at room temperature for up to 1 week.

Nutrition Facts per ½ cup: 145 cal., 8 g total fat (2 g sat. fat), 9 mg chol., 184 mg sodium, 16 g carbo. (1 g sugar), 1 g fiber, 4 g pro.
Exchanges: 1 Starch, 1½ Fat

get active

Ditch the car once in a while! Walk, jog, or bike to and from local places such as school, a neighbor's house, or the park.

GUACAMOLE-STUFFED TOMATOES

START TO FINISH: 20 minutes **MAKES:** 4 servings

- **4 medium tomatoes (about 6 ounces each)**
- **1 ripe avocado, halved, seeded, peeled, and chopped**
- **1 tablespoon finely chopped onion**
- **2 teaspoons snipped fresh cilantro**
- **2 teaspoons lemon juice**
- **1 small clove garlic, minced**
- **1/8 teaspoon salt**
- **2 ounces purchased baked tortilla chips**

ONE Cut a 1/4-inch slice from the stem end of each tomato. Using a spoon, carefully scoop out the tomato pulp, leaving a 1/4- to 1/2-inch-thick shell. Discard seeds. Set tomatoes cut side down on paper towels until ready to stuff. Chop enough of the tomato pulp to equal 1/3 cup; discard remaining pulp.

TWO In a medium bowl mash avocado slightly; stir in chopped tomato pulp, onion, cilantro, lemon juice, garlic, and salt. Divide avocado mixture among tomatoes, stuffing it into the shells. Serve with tortilla chips.

Nutrition Facts per serving: 204 cal., 6 g total fat (1 g sat. fat), 0 mg chol., 156 mg sodium, 22 g carbo. (5 g sugar), 5 g fiber, 4 g pro.
Exchanges: 1 Vegetable, 1 Starch, 1 1/2 Fat

VERY VEGGIE DIP

START TO FINISH: 20 minutes **MAKES:** 16 (2-tablespoon) servings dip

- **1 8-ounce carton light dairy sour cream**
- **½ of an 8-ounce package reduced-fat cream cheese (Neufchâtel)**
- **1 tablespoon milk**
- **¼ cup finely chopped red or yellow sweet pepper**
- **¼ cup finely chopped zucchini**
- **2 tablespoons shredded carrot**
- **1 tablespoon snipped fresh chives or green onion tops**
- **Salt and black pepper**
- **Cut-up vegetables, assorted crackers, and/or baked tortilla chips**

ONE In a medium mixing bowl beat sour cream, cream cheese, and milk with an electric mixer until smooth. Stir in sweet pepper, zucchini, carrot, and chives. Season to taste with salt and black pepper. Serve immediately or cover and chill for up to 3 days. Stir before serving. Serve with cut-up vegetables, crackers, and/or tortilla chips.

Nutrition Facts per serving: 39 cal., 3 g total fat (2 g sat. fat), 10 mg chol., 57 mg sodium, 1 g carbo. (1 g sugar), 0 g fiber, 2 g pro.
Exchanges: ½ Fat

ITALIAN VEGGIE DIP: Prepare as above except omit the sweet pepper, carrot, and chives. Stir in ¼ cup seeded and finely chopped tomato and 1 small clove garlic, minced. Stir in 1 tablespoon snipped fresh basil, oregano, and/or thyme or 1 teaspoon dried Italian seasoning, crushed. Makes 16 (2-tablespoon) servings.

Nutrition Facts per serving: 38 cal., 3 g fat (2 g sat. fat), 10 mg chol., 56 mg sodium, 1 g carbo. (1 g sugar), 0 g fiber, 2 g protein.
Exchanges: ½ Fat

SOUTH-OF-THE-BORDER VEGGIE DIP: Prepare as above except omit the sweet pepper, zucchini, carrot, and chives. Stir in ⅔ cup Easy Fresh Salsa (see recipe, page 121) or bottled salsa. Makes 16 (2-tablespoon) servings.

Nutrition Facts per serving: 39 cal., 3 g fat (2 g sat. fat), 10 mg chol., 60 mg sodium, 2 g carbo. (1 g sugar), 0 g fiber, 2 g protein.
Exchanges: ½ Fat

FAST, FRESH POTATO WEDGES

PREP: 10 minutes **BAKE:** 20 minutes **OVEN:** 425°F **MAKES:** 3 or 4 servings

Nonstick cooking spray

2 medium russet or Yukon gold potatoes

Salt and black pepper

ONE Lightly coat a large baking sheet with nonstick cooking spray; set aside. Scrub potatoes thoroughly with a brush; pat dry. If desired, peel potatoes. Cut each potato lengthwise into 8 wedges. Arrange potato wedges on prepared baking sheet. Coat potatoes lightly with cooking spray; sprinkle lightly with salt and pepper.

TWO Bake in a 425° oven for 20 to 25 minutes or until tender and golden brown, turning after 15 minutes. Transfer to a serving plate; cool slightly.

Nutrition Facts per serving: 74 cal., 0 g total fat (0 g sat. fat), 0 mg chol., 201 mg sodium, 17 g carbo. (5 g sugar), 2 g fiber, 2 g pro.
Exchanges: 1 Starch

get active

Go for a family camping trip—you can exercise by pitching a tent, gathering firewood, fishing, biking, and walking, all in one weekend.

WIGGLE CUPS

PREP: 20 minutes **STAND:** 30 minutes **CHILL:** 3 hours **MAKES:** 12 servings

2½ cups boiling water

3 4-serving-size packages desired flavor sugar-free gelatin

1 cup cold fat-free milk

1 4-serving-size package sugar-free instant vanilla-flavored pudding mix

ONE In a large bowl combine boiling water and gelatin; stir about 3 minutes or until gelatin is completely dissolved. Let stand for 30 minutes.

TWO In a medium bowl combine milk and pudding mix; beat with a wire whisk for 1 minute. Immediately stir into gelatin mixture, stirring with the wire whisk until well combined. Pour into twelve 2½-inch muffin cups. Cover and chill in the refrigerator for 3 hours or until set.

THREE Using a sharp small knife, loosen gelatin in muffin cups; remove gelatin treats from muffin cups.

Nutrition Facts per serving: 25 cal., 0 g total fat (0 g sat. fat), 0 mg chol., 189 mg sodium, 3 g carbo. (1 g sugar), 0 g fiber, 2 g pro.
Exchanges: Free

DOUBLE-DECKER FRUIT STACKS

START TO FINISH: 20 minutes **MAKES:** 4 servings

½ **of an 8-ounce tub light cream cheese, softened**

½ **teaspoon finely shredded orange peel**

2 **to 3 teaspoons fat-free milk**

3 **8-inch whole wheat or plain flour tortillas**

1 **medium apple, pear, and/or banana**

¼ **cup chopped almonds, pecans, or walnuts, toasted, if desired (optional)**

ONE In a small bowl stir together cream cheese, orange peel, and enough milk to make spreading consistency; set aside. Using a 3- to 3½-inch round cutter, cut tortillas into rounds (discard scraps). Spread tortilla rounds with cream cheese mixture; set aside. If using apple or pear, core and thinly slice crosswise. If using banana, peel and slice.

TWO On one-third of the tortilla rounds, arrange half of the fruit slices. If desired, sprinkle with half of the almonds. Top each with another tortilla round, cream cheese side up. Top with remaining fruit slices and, if desired, almonds. Top with remaining tortilla rounds, cream cheese side down.

Nutrition Facts per serving: 177 cal., 6 g total fat (3 g sat. fat), 13 mg chol., 419 mg sodium, 26 g carbo. (8 g sugar), 2 g fiber, 6 g pro.
Exchanges: ½ Fruit, 1 Starch, 1 Fat

FRUIT-FILLED WAFFLE CONES

START TO FINISH: 10 minutes **MAKES:** 4 servings

1 **4-serving-size package sugar-free instant lemon, vanilla, or white chocolate pudding mix**

1⅓ **cups fat-free milk**

1 **cup fresh fruit, such as blueberries, sliced kiwifruit, sliced strawberries, raspberries, or sliced bananas**

4 **waffle ice cream cones or large waffle ice cream bowls**

ONE Prepare pudding according to package directions using the 1⅓ cups milk. Spoon fruit into cones. Top with pudding. Serve immediately.

Nutrition Facts per serving: 143 cal., 1 g total fat (0 g sat. fat), 2 mg chol., 406 mg sodium, 29 g carbo. (11 g sugar), 2 g fiber, 4 g pro.
Exchanges: 2 Other Carbo.

get active

Take your physical activity to another level by planning an afternoon of kite flying.

cut the sugar

When compared to this homemade smoothie, you'll find that premade bottled smoothies have up to two and a half times the amount of sugar.

ICY MELON-BERRY SMOOTHIES

photo, p. 14–15

START TO FINISH: 15 minutes **MAKES:** 4 servings

- **1 cup frozen unsweetened whole strawberries**
- **1 cup cut-up cantaloupe**
- **⅓ cup orange juice**
- **¼ cup fat-free milk**
- **1 tablespoon honey**
- **1 cup ice cubes**

ONE In a blender container combine strawberries, cantaloupe, orange juice, milk, and honey. Cover and blend until smooth. Add ice cubes; cover and blend until smooth. Pour into glasses.

TIP: If desired, omit the honey and sweeten to taste with desired artificial sweetener.

Nutrition Facts per serving: 57 cal., 0 g total fat (0 g sat. fat), 0 mg chol., 15 mg sodium, 14 g carbo. (10 g sugar), 1 g fiber, 1 g pro.
Exchanges: 1 Fruit

PEACH SHAKES

START TO FINISH: 10 minutes **MAKES:** 3 servings

2 cups frozen unsweetened peach slices

1¾ cups fat-free milk

1 tablespoon honey

1 teaspoon vanilla

ONE In a blender container combine frozen peach slices, milk, honey, and vanilla. Cover and blend until smooth. Pour into glasses.

Nutrition Facts per serving: 145 cal., 3 g total fat (2 g sat. fat), 0 mg chol., 0 mg sodium, 0 g carbo. (22 g sugar), 2 g fiber, 5 g pro.
Exchanges: ½ Milk, 1 Fruit

FRUIT SMOOTHIES

START TO FINISH: 10 minutes **MAKES:** 4 servings

2 **8-ounce cartons fat-free plain yogurt**

2 **ripe small bananas**

1 **cup sliced fresh strawberries or unsweetened frozen strawberries**

1 **cup fresh mixed berries, such as raspberries, blueberries, and/or blackberries, or unsweetened frozen mixed berries**

ONE In a blender container combine yogurt, bananas, and berries; cover and blend until smooth.

Nutrition Facts per serving: 125 cal., 1 g total fat (0 g sat. fat), 2 mg chol., 88 mg sodium, 24 g carbo. (17 g sugar), 3 g fiber, 7 g pro.
Exchanges: 1 Milk, 1 Fruit

cut the sugar

If using frozen strawberries, choose unsweetened berries. Sweetened frozen strawberries have as much as four times the amount of sugar per serving.

FRUITY ICED TEA

PREP: 15 minutes **STAND:** 3 minutes **MAKES:** 8 to 10 servings

6 bags wild berry-flavored tea

3 cups boiling water

1 tub low-calorie pineapple-orange-flavored or orange-flavored soft drink mix ($\frac{1}{2}$ of 1.2-ounce can or $\frac{1}{4}$ of 1.5-ounce can)

5 cups cold water

Ice cubes

ONE Place tea bags in a 2-quart clear glass container. Pour boiling water over tea bags. Cover and let stand about 3 minutes. Remove tea bags; discard. Add drink mix, stirring to dissolve. Add cold water; stir. Serve over ice cubes. Store leftover tea in the refrigerator.

ROSY-RED CRANBERRY TEA: Place 6 bags cranberry-apple-flavored tea in a 2-quart clear glass container. Pour 3 cups boiling water over tea bags. Cover and let stand about 3 minutes. Remove tea bags; discard. Add 1 tub low-calorie pink lemonade-flavored soft drink mix ($\frac{1}{4}$ of a 1.9-ounce can or $\frac{1}{6}$ of a 2.9-ounce can), stirring to dissolve. Add cold water; stir. Serve over ice cubes. Store leftover tea in the refrigerator.

Nutrition Facts per serving: 75 cal., 0 g total fat (0 g sat. fat), 0 mg chol., 7 mg sodium, 1 g carbo. (0 g sugar), 0 g fiber, 0 g pro.
Exchanges: Free

cut the sugar

A serving of Fruity Iced Tea or Rosy-Red Cranberry Tea contains no sugar, while store-bought prepared mixes have on average 16.5 grams of sugar in each serving.

BUBBLY **CITRUS** COOLER

PREP: 10 minutes **MAKES:** 10 to 12 servings

1 **envelope (0.28-ounce) low-calorie cherry- or punch-flavored soft drink mix**

1 **cup orange juice**

1 **2-liter bottle carbonated water, chilled**

Ice cubes

ONE In a large pitcher combine drink mix and orange juice. Add carbonated water. Stir to dissolve drink mix. Serve immediately over ice cubes.

TO MAKE I SERVING: Stir together drink mix and orange juice and keep in a covered container in the refrigerator for up to 1 week. Add 4 to 5 teaspoons of the orange juice mixture to $^3/_4$ to 1 cup of carbonated water; stir to combine. Serve over ice cubes.

Nutrition Facts per serving: 15 cal., 0 g total fat (0 g sat. fat), 0 mg chol., 46 mg sodium, 3 g carbo. (0 g sugar), 0 g fiber, 0 g pro.
Exchanges: Free

wake up, s

Pancakes with apples, waffles with pumpkin, muffins with oats, granola with bran cereal—now these are worth getting out of bed for. Whatever your kids like in the morning, we've got you covered.

eepyhead

get active

This weekend stage your own "Olympic Games" complete with sack races, three-legged races, and beanbag tosses.

APPLE GRIDDLE CAKES

PREP: 25 minutes **COOK:** 2 minutes per batch **MAKES:** 8 servings

- **2 large cooking apples, such as Jonathan or Granny Smith, peeled, if desired, and finely chopped (about 1½ cups)**
- **2 teaspoons lemon juice**
- **1½ cups whole wheat flour**
- **2 tablespoons sugar**
- **2 teaspoons baking powder**
- **½ teaspoon ground cinnamon**
- **¼ teaspoon salt**
- **1 slightly beaten egg**
- **1½ cups milk**
- **3 tablespoons cooking oil or melted butter**
- **Cooking oil (optional)**
- **Unsweetened applesauce (optional)**

ONE In a medium bowl combine apples and lemon juice. In another medium bowl combine flour, sugar, baking powder, cinnamon, and salt. In a small bowl combine egg, milk, and oil.

TWO Add egg mixture all at once to flour mixture; stir just until moistened (the batter should be lumpy). Gently fold in apple mixture.

THREE Heat a lightly greased griddle or heavy skillet over medium heat until a few drops of water dance across the surface. For each pancake, pour a scant ¼ cup batter onto the hot griddle; spread batter into a 4-inch circle.

FOUR Cook for 1 to 2 minutes on each side or until pancakes are golden, turning to second sides when pancake surfaces are bubbly and edges are slightly dry, adding oil to griddle as necessary. Serve warm. If desired, top with applesauce.

Nutrition Facts per serving: 184 cal., 7 g total fat (1 g sat. fat), 30 mg chol., 164 mg sodium, 27 g carbo. (9 g sugar), 4 g fiber, 5 g pro.
Exchanges: ½ Fruit, 1 Starch, ½ Other Carbo., 1 Fat

THREE-GRAIN FLAPJACKS

PREP: 15 minutes **COOK:** 3 minutes per batch **STAND:** 10 minutes **MAKES:** 8 to 10 servings

1½ cups all-purpose flour

½ cup yellow cornmeal

2½ teaspoons baking powder

½ teaspoon salt

½ cup regular rolled oats

3 tablespoons packed brown sugar

1 beaten egg

1¾ cups fat-free milk

¼ cup low-fat plain yogurt

3 tablespoons cooking oil

½ cup dried blueberries or currants (optional)

Nonstick cooking spray

Unsweetened applesauce (optional)

ONE In a large bowl stir together flour, cornmeal, baking powder, and salt. In a blender container or food processor bowl combine oats and brown sugar. Cover and blend or process until oats are coarsely ground. Stir oat mixture into flour mixture. Make a well in the center of flour mixture.

TWO In a medium bowl combine egg, milk, yogurt, and oil. Add egg mixture all at once to flour mixture. Stir just until moistened (batter should be lumpy and thin). Let stand for 10 minutes to thicken slightly, stirring once or twice. If desired, gently fold in blueberries.

THREE Lightly coat an unheated nonstick griddle or heavy skillet with nonstick cooking spray. Heat over medium heat. For silver-dollar-size pancakes, pour or spread about 1 tablespoon batter into a 1-inch circle onto hot griddle or skillet. For standard-size pancakes, pour or spread about ¼ cup batter into a 3-inch circle onto hot griddle or skillet. Cook over medium heat for 1½ to 2 minutes on each side or until pancakes are golden brown, turning to second sides when pancake surfaces are bubbly and edges are slightly dry. Serve warm. If desired, top with applesauce.

Nutrition Facts per serving: 232 cal., 7 g total fat (1 g sat. fat), 28 mg chol., 261 mg sodium, 36 g carbo. (9 g sugar), 2 g fiber, 7 g pro.
Exchanges: 1½ Starch, 1 Other Carbo., 1 Fat

PUMPKIN WAFFLES

PREP: 10 minutes **BAKE:** per manufacturer's directions **MAKES:** 10 servings

- **2 cups all-purpose flour**
- **2 tablespoons brown sugar**
- **1 tablespoon baking powder**
- **½ teaspoon salt**
- **½ teaspoon pumpkin pie spice**
- **1½ cups fat-free milk**
- **1 cup canned pumpkin**
- **2 slightly beaten eggs**
- **2 tablespoons cooking oil**
- **Orange sections (optional)**

ONE In a medium bowl stir together flour, brown sugar, baking powder, salt, and pumpkin pie spice. Make a well in the center of the flour mixture.

TWO In another medium bowl combine milk, pumpkin, eggs, and oil. Add milk mixture all at once to flour mixture; stir just until moistened (the batter should be lumpy).

THREE Pour about ¾ cup batter onto grids of a preheated, lightly greased waffle baker. Close lid quickly; do not open until done. Bake according to manufacturer's directions. When done, use a fork to lift waffle off grids. Repeat with remaining batter. Serve warm. If desired, top with orange sections.

Nutrition Facts per serving: 155 cal., 4 g total fat (1 g sat. fat), 43 mg chol., 221 mg sodium, 24 g carbo. (6 g sugar), 1 g fiber, 5 g pro.
Exchanges: 1 Starch, ½ Other Carbo., ½ Fat

APPLE-CHERRY-FILLED ROLLS

PREP: 30 minutes **RISE:** 30 minutes **BAKE:** 13 minutes **OVEN:** 375°F **MAKES:** 16 rolls

Nonstick cooking spray

1 **16-ounce package hot roll mix**

1 **cup chopped, cored apple**

¼ **cup dried cherries or golden raisins**

½ **teaspoon ground cinnamon**

ONE Lightly coat 2 baking sheets with nonstick cooking spray; set aside.

TWO Prepare hot roll mix according to package directions through the resting step. Meanwhile, for filling, in a small bowl stir together apple, dried cherries, and cinnamon.

THREE Divide dough into 16 portions. Flatten one portion of dough into a 3-inch circle; spoon 1 rounded teaspoon of filling onto dough. Shape dough around the filling to enclose it, pulling dough until smooth and rounded. Place roll, rounded side up, on the prepared baking sheet. Repeat with remaining dough and filling. Cover; let rise until nearly double in size (about 30 minutes).

FOUR Bake in a 375° oven for 13 to 15 minutes or until golden. Cool slightly on a wire rack. Serve warm.

Nutrition Facts per roll: 131 cal., 2 g total fat (0 g sat. fat), 13 mg chol., 185 mg sodium, 24 g carbo. (1 g sugar), 0 g fiber, 4 g pro.
Exchanges: 1 Starch, ½ Other Carbo.

BANANA OAT MUFFINS

PREP: 20 minutes **BAKE:** 20 minutes **OVEN:** 350°F **MAKES:** 12 muffins

Paper bake cups

2 cups regular rolled oats

³/₄ cup whole wheat flour

¹/₃ cup sugar

1 teaspoon baking powder

³/₄ teaspoon apple pie spice
or ground cinnamon

¹/₂ teaspoon baking soda

¹/₂ teaspoon salt

1 cup buttermilk

1 large ripe banana, mashed

2 slightly beaten eggs

2 tablespoons butter, melted

1 teaspoon vanilla

¹/₄ cup regular rolled oats

¹/₂ teaspoon apple pie spice
or ground cinnamon

1 tablespoon butter

ONE Line twelve 2¹/₂-inch muffin cups with paper bake cups. Place 2 cups rolled oats in a food processor bowl or blender container; cover and process or blend until fine. Transfer oats to a large bowl; stir in whole wheat flour, sugar, baking powder, ³/₄ teaspoon apple pie spice, baking soda, and salt. Make a well in the center of the flour mixture; set aside.

TWO In a medium bowl whisk together buttermilk, banana, eggs, 2 tablespoons butter, and vanilla. Add buttermilk mixture all at once to flour mixture; stir just until moistened. Spoon batter into muffin cups.

THREE For topping, stir together ¹/₄ cup oats and ¹/₂ teaspoon apple pie spice. Cut in 1 tablespoon butter until mixture is crumbly. Sprinkle tops with oat mixture.

FOUR Bake in a 350° oven for 20 to 22 minutes or until a toothpick inserted in centers of muffins comes out clean.

MAKE-AHEAD: Store baked muffins in an airtight container at room temperature for up to 3 days. Freeze for up to 1 month.

Nutrition Facts per muffin: 174 cal., 5 g total fat (2 g sat. fat), 44 mg chol., 225 mg sodium, 27 g carbo. (8 g sugar), 3 g fiber, 6 g pro.
Exchanges: 1 ½ Starch, ½ Other Carbo., ½ Fat

FRUITY POCKET TARTS

PREP: 45 minutes **BAKE:** 14 minutes **OVEN:** 375°F **MAKES:** 16 tarts

3 cups whole wheat pastry flour

2 cups all-purpose flour

1 teaspoon salt

$\frac{1}{2}$ teaspoon apple pie spice, ground cinnamon, or ground cardamom

$1\frac{1}{3}$ cups shortening

$\frac{3}{4}$ to 1 cup cold water

4 medium apples, peeled, if desired, cored, and chopped, or 4 cups blueberries

$\frac{1}{4}$ cup packed brown sugar

1 tablespoon all-purpose flour

1 teaspoon apple pie spice, ground cinnamon, or ground cardamom

Milk

ONE In a medium bowl stir together whole wheat flour, 2 cups all-purpose flour, salt, and $\frac{1}{2}$ teaspoon apple pie spice. Using a pastry blender, cut in shortening until pieces are the size of small peas. Sprinkle 2 tablespoons of water over part of the mixture. Gently toss with a fork. Push moistened part to side of bowl. Repeat until all dough is moistened. Form dough into a ball. Divide dough into 4 equal portions.

TWO On a lightly floured surface, roll one portion of the dough into an 11-inch square. Cut into four $5\frac{1}{2}$-inch squares. In a medium bowl combine apples, brown sugar, 1 tablespoon all-purpose flour, and 1 teaspoon apple pie spice. Place $\frac{1}{4}$ cup of the fruit mixture on half of each square of dough, leaving a $\frac{1}{2}$-inch border on the edges.

THREE Moisten edges of squares with a little milk. Fold dough up over filling to make a rectangle. Use the tines of a fork to press edges to seal.

FOUR Place tarts on foil-lined baking sheets and make small slashes in the tops to allow steam to escape. Lightly brush with milk. Repeat with remaining dough and fruit mixture. Bake in a 375° oven for 14 to 18 minutes or until edges are golden brown. Transfer to a wire rack. Serve warm or cool.

MAKE-AHEAD: Prepare tarts as directed. Wrap cooled tarts individually in plastic wrap. Place tarts in a large self-sealing plastic bag. Freeze for up to 3 months. Thaw tarts in the refrigerator. To reheat, place tarts on a baking sheet. Bake in a 350°F oven for 10 minutes or until heated through.

Nutrition Facts per tart: 294 cal., 18 g total fat (4 g sat. fat), 0 mg chol., 148 mg sodium, 32 g carbo. (7 g sugar), 3 g fiber, 4 g pro.
Exchanges: 1 Starch, 1 Other Carbo., 3$\frac{1}{2}$ Fat

STRAWBERRY-BANANA BREAD

PREP: 15 minutes **BAKE:** per bread machine directions **MAKES:** one 1½-pound loaf (16 servings)

⅓ **cup fat-free milk**

⅓ **cup mashed ripe banana (1 medium)**

¼ **cup low-sugar strawberry preserves (with no artificial sweetener)**

1 **egg**

2 **tablespoons butter or margarine, cut up**

1 **tablespoon water**

3 **cups bread flour**

¾ **teaspoon salt**

1 **teaspoon active dry yeast or bread machine yeast**

½ **cup chopped pecans, toasted (optional)**

ONE Add all ingredients to a 1½- or 2-pound bread machine according to the manufacturer's directions. Select the basic white bread cycle and desired color setting for a 1½-pound loaf.

Nutrition Facts per serving: 126 cal., 2 g total fat (1 g sat. fat), 17 mg chol., 127 mg sodium, 22 g carbo. (3 g sugar), 1 g fiber, 4 g pro.
Exchanges: 1 Starch, ½ Other Carbo., ½ Fat

cut the sugar

A store-bought banana bread mix may have up to 12 grams of sugar per serving, but this recipe has 3 grams per serving.

EASY **STRAWBERRY-APPLE** FREEZER JAM

PREP: 30 minutes **STAND:** 24 hours **MAKES:** 6 half pints

6 **cups strawberries, washed and hulled (about 1³/₄ pounds)**

1 **cup finely shredded, peeled apple (about 2 medium)**

1 **teaspoon finely shredded orange peel**

3 **cups sugar**

1 **1³/₄-ounce package powdered fruit pectin for lower sugar recipes**

1 **cup water**

ONE In a large bowl use a potato masher to crush strawberries thoroughly (you should have 3 cups). Stir in apple and orange peel. Set aside.

TWO In a large saucepan combine sugar and pectin. Stir in water. Bring to boiling over medium-high heat, stirring constantly. Cook and stir for 1 minute. Remove from heat. Add strawberry mixture. Stir for 1 minute or until well combined.

THREE Ladle into clean half-pint freezer containers, leaving a ¹/₂-inch headspace. Seal and label. Let stand at room temperature for 24 hours or until set. Store for up to 3 weeks in the refrigerator or for up to 1 year in the freezer.

Nutrition Facts per 1 tablespoon: 32 cal., 0 g total fat (0 g sat. fat), 0 mg chol., 3 mg sodium, 9 g carbo. (8 g sugar), 0 g fiber, 0 g pro. **Exchanges:** ¹/₂ Other Carbo.

HONEY-ORANGE GRANOLA

PREP: 15 minutes **BAKE:** 30 minutes **OVEN:** 325°F **MAKES:** 12 servings

Nonstick cooking spray

2½ **cups regular rolled oats**

1 **cup wheat flakes**

⅓ **cup Grape-Nuts or whole bran cereal**

⅓ **cup sliced almonds or pecan pieces**

⅓ **cup orange juice**

2 **tablespoons honey**

¼ **teaspoon ground allspice**

¼ **teaspoon ground cinnamon**

Low-fat yogurt, fat-free milk, or fresh fruit (optional)

ONE Coat a 15X10X1-inch baking pan with nonstick cooking spray; set aside. In a large bowl stir together oats, wheat flakes, Grape-Nuts, and nuts. In a small saucepan stir together juice, honey, allspice, and cinnamon. Cook and stir just until boiling. Remove from heat. Pour over oat mixture, tossing just until coated.

TWO Spread oat mixture evenly in prepared pan. Bake, uncovered, in a 325° oven for 30 to 35 minutes or until oats are lightly browned, stirring twice. Remove from oven. Turn out onto a large piece of foil; cool completely. If desired, serve with yogurt, milk, or fresh fruit.

MAKE-AHEAD: Prepare as directed. Store in an airtight container in the refrigerator for up to 2 weeks or in the freezer for up to 3 months.

Nutrition Facts per ⅓ cup: 136 cal., 3 g total fat (0 g sat. fat), 0 mg chol., 39 mg sodium, 23 g carbo. (4 g sugar), 3 g fiber, 4 g pro.
Exchanges: 1 Starch, ½ Other Carbo., ½ Fat

cut the sugar

Regular boxed granola can have anywhere from 9 to 13 grams of sugar per serving. This homemade granola has less than 4 grams per serving.

CREAMY FRUIT DIP

photo, p. 34–35

START TO FINISH: 15 minutes **MAKES:** about 2⅓ cups

1 **cup sliced, peeled peaches; strawberries; mandarin orange sections; or cubed fresh pineapple**

1 **8-ounce carton light dairy sour cream**

1 **8-ounce package reduced-fat cream cheese (Neufchâtel)**

½ **teaspoon finely shredded orange peel**

1 **teaspoon vanilla**

ONE Place fruit in a blender container or food processor bowl. Cover and blend or process until smooth. Add sour cream, cream cheese, orange peel, and vanilla. Cover and blend or process until smooth. Serve immediately or cover and chill for up to 24 hours. (If dip is too thick after chilling, stir in fat-free milk, 1 tablespoon at a time, to reach desired consistency).

Nutrition Facts per 1 tablespoon: 26 cal., 2 g total fat (1 g sat. fat), 7 mg chol., 28 mg sodium, 1 g carbo. (0 g sugar), 0 g fiber, 1 g pro.
Exchanges: ½ Fat

APPLE-CINNAMON DIP: Prepare as above except omit the 1 cup fruit and the orange peel. Add ½ cup unsweetened applesauce and ¼ to ½ teaspoon apple pie spice or ground cinnamon with the vanilla. Makes about 2 cups.

Nutrition Facts per 1 tablespoon: 29 cal., 2 g total fat (1 g sat. fat), 8 mg chol., 33 g sodium, 1 g carbo. (1 g sugar), 0 g fiber, 1 g pro.
Exchanges: ½ Fat

PEANUT BUTTER DIP: Prepare as above except omit the 1 cup fruit and the orange peel. Add ½ cup creamy peanut butter with the sour cream and 2 to 4 tablespoons of milk to reach desired consistency. Makes about 2½ cups.

Nutrition Facts per 1 tablespoon: 42 cal., 3 g total fat (1 g sat. fat), 6 mg chol., 42 g sodium, 1 g carbo. (1 g sugar), 0 g fiber, 2 g pro.
Exchanges: 1 Fat

EGG-BACON POCKETS

START TO FINISH: 15 minutes **MAKES:** 4 servings

2 **eggs**

4 **egg whites**

3 **ounces Canadian-style bacon, chopped**

3 **tablespoons water**

2 **tablespoons sliced green onion (optional)**

$\frac{1}{8}$ **teaspoon salt**

Nonstick cooking spray

2 **large whole wheat pita bread rounds, halved crosswise**

$\frac{1}{2}$ **cup shredded reduced-fat cheddar cheese (2 ounces) (optional)**

ONE In a medium bowl combine eggs, egg whites, bacon, water, green onion, if desired, and salt. Mix well with a wire whisk or rotary beater until blended.

TWO Lightly coat an unheated large nonstick skillet with nonstick cooking spray. Heat over medium heat. Add egg mixture to skillet. Cook, without stirring, until mixture begins to set on the bottom and around the edge. Using a spatula or a large spoon, lift and fold the partially cooked eggs so the uncooked portion flows underneath. Continue cooking about 2 minutes or until egg mixture is cooked through but is still glossy and moist. Remove from heat.

THREE Fill pita halves with egg mixture. If desired, sprinkle with cheese.

Nutrition Facts per serving: 162 cal., 4 g total fat (1 g sat. fat), 118 mg chol., 616 mg sodium, 18 g carbo. (1 g sugar), 2 g fiber, 13 g pro.
Exchanges: 1 Starch, 1$\frac{1}{2}$ Very Lean Meat, $\frac{1}{2}$ Fat

HAM AND CHEESE QUESADILLAS

START TO FINISH: 20 minutes **MAKES:** 4 servings

- ³/₄ cup shredded Swiss, Monterey Jack, or cheddar cheese (3 ounces)
- 4 7- to 8-inch whole wheat, spinach, tomato, or plain flour tortillas
- 3 ounces thinly sliced cooked ham
- ²/₃ cup chopped tomato
- 2 tablespoons sliced green onion tops (optional)

ONE Sprinkle cheese over half of each tortilla. Top with ham, tomato, and, if desired, green onion tops. Fold tortillas in half, pressing together gently.

TWO In a 10-inch skillet cook quesadillas, 2 at a time, over medium heat for 1½ to 2 minutes per side or until lightly browned. Cut quesadillas into wedges and serve immediately.

Nutrition Facts per serving: 260 cal., 10 g total fat (5 g sat. fat), 31 mg chol., 699 mg sodium, 29 g carbo. (4 g sugar), 3 g fiber, 13 g pro.
Exchanges: 2 Starch, 1 Lean Meat, 1 Fat

get active

Grab a boomerang and take turns throwing it around the yard. Run after it instead of waiting for it to come back to you.

BREAKFAST TACOS

START TO FINISH: 20 minutes **MAKES:** 8 to 10 servings

Nonstick cooking spray

⅓ cup chopped celery

⅓ cup chopped green sweet pepper

1 cup chopped cooked ham

1 8-ounce can crushed pineapple (juice pack), well drained, or ¾ cup finely chopped apple

1 cup shredded cheddar cheese (4 ounces)

8 to 10 6-inch whole wheat or plain flour tortillas, warmed

ONE Lightly coat a small nonstick skillet with cooking spray. Heat skillet over medium heat. Cook celery and sweet pepper in hot skillet until tender, stirring occasionally. Stir in ham and pineapple. Cook and stir until heated through. Remove from heat. Stir in cheese.

TWO Spoon about ¼ cup filling in the center of each warmed tortilla. Roll up tortillas.

TO WARM TORTILLAS: Wrap tortillas tightly in foil. Heat in a 350°F oven about 10 minutes or until heated through.

Nutrition Facts per serving: 182 cal., 8 g total fat (4 g sat. fat), 25 mg chol., 526 mg sodium, 20 g carbo. (6 g sugar), 2 g fiber, 9 g pro.
Exchanges: 1 Starch, 1 Medium-Fat Meat, ½ Fat

BACON AND CHEESE TURNOVERS

PREP: 30 minutes **BAKE:** 12 minutes **OVEN:** 400°F **MAKES:** 9 turnovers

- **1 10-ounce package refrigerated pizza dough**
- **2 tablespoons low-sugar orange marmalade**
- **3/4 cup chopped Canadian-style bacon or cooked ham**
- **3/4 cup shredded Swiss cheese (3 ounces)**
- **1/4 cup thinly sliced green onions**
- **Freshly ground black pepper**
- **Milk**
- **Poppy seeds and/or sesame seeds**

ONE Line a baking sheet with foil; grease foil. Set aside. Unroll pizza dough onto a lightly floured surface. Roll dough into a 12-inch square. Spread orange marmalade evenly over dough. Cut dough into nine 4-inch squares.

TWO For filling, in a medium bowl stir together bacon, cheese, and green onions. Place about 3 tablespoons filling on each dough square. Sprinkle each lightly with pepper. Fold one corner of each dough square over filling to opposite corner. Use the tines of a fork to press edges to seal. Prick tops of turnovers with the fork.

THREE Place turnovers on prepared baking sheet. Brush with milk and sprinkle with poppy seeds and/or sesame seeds. Bake in a 400° oven for 12 to 15 minutes or until golden (filling will leak out slightly). Serve warm.

Nutrition Facts per turnover: 127 cal., 5 g total fat (2 g sat. fat), 14 mg chol., 275 mg sodium, 14 g carbo. (1 g sugar), 1 g fiber, 7 g pro.
Exchanges: 1 Starch, 1/2 Medium-Fat Meat, 1/2 Fat

cut the sugar

Instead of serving your kids a sugary pastry for breakfast, try these savory turnovers, which are low in fat and sugar.

soup

or salad?

Most kids love soup, but with prepared soups you often get hidden sugars, sodium, and not much else. Make your own with a mix of vegetables, chicken, pasta, and other basic ingredients. If the kids want some crunch, give them one of these fun, colorful salads.

SOUPER WHEELIES 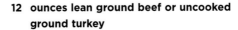 photo, p. 54

PREP: 30 minutes **COOK:** 22 minutes **MAKES:** 4 servings

12 ounces lean ground beef or uncooked
   ground turkey

1 small onion, chopped (¹/₃ cup)

1 14-ounce can beef broth

1¹/₂ cups water

³/₄ cup dried wagon wheel pasta

1 cup frozen whole kernel corn

1 cup frozen cut green beans

1 teaspoon dried basil, crushed

¹/₂ teaspoon dried oregano, crushed

1 14¹/₂-ounce can Italian-style stewed
   tomatoes, undrained

ONE In a large saucepan cook beef and
onion over medium-high heat until beef is
no longer pink and onion is tender. Drain.

TWO Add broth and water to beef mixture.
Bring mixture to boiling over high heat. Add
pasta. Reduce heat to medium-high. Cook,
uncovered, for 12 minutes. Stir in corn, green
beans, basil, oregano, and undrained
tomatoes. Return to boiling; reduce heat
to medium-low. Cook, covered, about
10 minutes or until vegetables are tender.

Nutrition Facts per serving: 316 cal., 10 g total fat
(3 g sat. fat), 55 mg chol., 623 mg sodium, 35 g carbo.
(9 g sugar), 4 g fiber, 22 g pro.
Exchanges: 1 Vegetable, 2 Starch, 2 Lean Meat, ¹/₂ Fat

get active

Use an active outing—a trip
to the park or the pool—as
a reward for good behavior
instead of sugar-filled candy.

ITALIAN MEATBALL SOUP

START TO FINISH: 25 minutes **MAKES:** 4 servings

- 1 14$\frac{1}{2}$-ounce can diced tomatoes with onion and garlic, undrained
- 1 14-ounce can reduced-sodium beef broth
- 1$\frac{1}{2}$ cups water
- $\frac{1}{2}$ teaspoon dried Italian seasoning, crushed
- $\frac{1}{2}$ of a 16-ounce package frozen Italian-style cooked meatballs
- $\frac{1}{2}$ cup small dried pasta, such as tripolini, ditalini, stellini, or orzo
- 1 cup loose-pack frozen mixed vegetables
- 1 tablespoon shredded or grated Parmesan cheese (optional)

ONE In a large saucepan stir together undrained tomatoes, broth, water, and Italian seasoning. Bring to boiling. Add meatballs, pasta, and frozen vegetables. Return to boiling; reduce heat. Simmer, covered, about 10 minutes or until pasta and vegetables are tender. If desired, sprinkle servings with cheese.

Nutrition Facts per serving: 283 cal., 13 g total fat (6 g sat. fat), 37 mg chol., 866 mg sodium, 27 g carbo. (3 g sugar), 5 g fiber, 14 g pro.
Exchanges: 1$\frac{1}{2}$ Vegetable, 1 Starch, 1$\frac{1}{2}$ Medium-Fat Meat, 1 Fat

PIZZA SOUP

1 **cup chopped onion**

1 **cup chopped green sweet pepper**

1 **cup sliced fresh mushrooms**

1 **cup halved, sliced zucchini**

1 **14-ounce can beef broth**

1 **14½-ounce can diced tomatoes with basil, garlic, and oregano, undrained**

1 **8-ounce can tomato sauce with garlic and onion**

4 **ounces cooked smoked turkey sausage, thinly sliced**

½ **teaspoon pizza seasoning, crushed**

½ **cup shredded reduced-fat mozzarella cheese (2 ounces)**

ONE In a medium saucepan combine onion, sweet pepper, mushrooms, zucchini, and ¼ cup of the broth. Bring to boiling; reduce heat. Simmer, covered, for 5 minutes.

TWO Stir in remaining broth, undrained tomatoes, tomato sauce, sausage, and pizza seasoning. Simmer, covered, for 5 to 10 minutes more or until vegetables are tender. Top each serving with cheese.

Nutrition Facts per serving: 119 cal., 3 g total fat (1 g sat. fat), 17 mg chol., 1,018 mg sodium, 14 g carbo. (7 g sugar), 2 g fiber, 9 g pro.
Exchanges: 1 Vegetable, ½ Other Carbo., 1 Lean Meat

cut the sugar

Canned soups often contain added sugar. This quick-to-make Pizza Soup has about half the sugar of a comparable canned soup.

TEXAS CHILI MADE EASY

START TO FINISH: 20 minutes **MAKES:** 6 servings

- **12 ounces lean ground beef**
- **1 15-ounce can pinto beans, undrained**
- **1 cup Easy Fresh Salsa (see recipe, page 121) or purchased bottled salsa**
- **½ cup beef broth**
- **1 teaspoon chili powder**
- **½ teaspoon ground cumin**
- **Texas toast (optional)**

ONE In a large skillet cook beef over medium heat until brown. Drain off fat. Add undrained beans, Easy Fresh Salsa, broth, chili powder, and cumin to skillet. Bring to boiling; reduce heat. Simmer, covered, for 10 minutes. If desired, serve with Texas toast.

Nutrition Facts per serving: 167 cal., 6 g total fat (2 g sat. fat), 36 mg chol., 278 mg sodium, 14 g carbo. (2 g sugar), 4 g fiber, 14 g pro.
Exchanges: 1 Starch, 1½ Lean Meat

cut the sugar

This chili has slightly more than 2 grams of sugar per serving. Store-bought canned chili can have 6 grams of sugar or more per serving.

SNOWBALL SOUP

START TO FINISH: 30 minutes **MAKES:** 6 servings

5 cups reduced-sodium chicken broth

2 medium carrots, sliced

2 stalks celery, chopped

$\frac{1}{8}$ teaspoon black pepper

1$\frac{1}{2}$ cups chopped cooked chicken

1$\frac{1}{2}$ cups packaged biscuit mix

$\frac{1}{2}$ cup milk

ONE In a medium saucepan combine broth, carrots, celery, and pepper. Bring to boiling; reduce heat. Simmer, covered, for 10 minutes. Stir in chicken.

TWO Meanwhile, in a medium bowl combine biscuit mix and milk. Stir just until combined.

THREE For dumplings, spoon dough in 12 mounds on top of hot broth mixture. Cook, covered, for 10 minutes more or until a toothpick inserted into dumplings comes out clean.

Nutrition Facts per serving: 222 cal., 8 g total fat (2 g sat. fat), 33 mg chol., 916 mg sodium, 23 g carbo. (4 g sugar), 1 g fiber, 15 g pro.
Exchanges: $\frac{1}{2}$ Vegetable, 1$\frac{1}{2}$ Starch, 1$\frac{1}{2}$ Lean Meat, $\frac{1}{2}$ Fat

CHICKEN TORTILLA SOUP

START TO FINISH: 20 minutes **MAKES:** 4 servings

- **2 14-ounce cans chicken broth**
- **2 cups loose-pack frozen pepper stir-fry vegetables (yellow, green, and red sweet peppers, and onions)**
- **1 14½-ounce can Mexican-style stewed tomatoes, undrained**
- **2 cups chopped cooked chicken**
- **1 cup crushed packaged baked tortilla chips (about 2 cups uncrushed)**
- **Light dairy sour cream, chopped avocado, and/or fresh cilantro sprig (optional)**

ONE In a large saucepan combine broth, frozen vegetables, and undrained tomatoes. Bring to boiling; reduce heat. Simmer, covered, for 3 to 5 minutes or until vegetables are tender. Stir in chicken; heat through.

TWO Ladle soup into warm soup bowls and sprinkle with crushed tortilla chips. If desired, top with sour cream, avocado, and/or cilantro.

Nutrition Facts per serving: 247 cal., 6 g total fat (1 g sat. fat), 64 mg chol., 1,266 mg sodium, 17 g carbo. (1 g sugar), 2 g fiber, 24 g pro.
Exchanges: 1½ Vegetable, ½ Other Carbo., 3 Very Lean Meat, 1 Fat

CHOOSE-A-VEGETABLE CHICKEN AND PASTA SOUP

START TO FINISH: 40 minutes **MAKES:** 6 servings

2 **14-ounce cans reduced-sodium chicken broth**

2 **cups water**

¼ **teaspoon black pepper**

1 **cup dried twisted spaghetti (gemelli) or broken fusilli**

3 **cups vegetables, such as thinly sliced carrots, small broccoli florets, chopped green or red sweet peppers, and/or fresh or frozen whole kernel corn**

1½ **cups cubed cooked chicken (about 8 ounces)**

1 **tablespoon snipped fresh basil**

¼ **cup finely shredded Parmesan cheese (1 ounce)**

ONE In a Dutch oven combine broth, water, and black pepper; bring to boiling. Stir in pasta. Return to boiling; reduce heat. Simmer, covered, for 5 minutes. Stir in vegetables. Return to boiling; reduce heat. Simmer, covered, for 5 to 8 minutes more or until vegetables and pasta are tender. Stir in chicken and basil; heat through. To serve, top with Parmesan cheese.

Nutrition Facts per serving: 172 cal., 4 g total fat (2 g sat. fat), 35 mg chol., 447 mg sodium, 18 g carbo. (5 g sugar), 2 g fiber, 16 g pro.
Exchanges: 1 Vegetable, 1 Starch, 1½ Lean Meat

get active

Use your favorite music—country western, hip-hop, or whatever—to hold a dance contest in your neighborhood.

MACARONI AND CHEESE CHOWDER

START TO FINISH: 30 minutes **MAKES:** 4 to 6 servings

1 **14-ounce can reduced-sodium chicken broth**

1 **cup water**

1 **cup dried elbow macaroni**

1 **cup frozen whole kernel corn**

1 **cup chopped low-fat thinly sliced cooked ham (5 ounces)**

6 **ounces American cheese, cubed**

1 **cup fat-free milk**

Shredded cheddar cheese (optional)

ONE In a large saucepan bring chicken broth and water to boiling. Add macaroni. Reduce heat to medium-low. Simmer, covered, for 12 minutes or until macaroni is tender, stirring occasionally.

TWO Stir in corn, ham, cheese, and milk. Cook and stir over medium heat until cheese melts. Ladle into bowls. If desired, top each serving with cheddar cheese.

Nutrition Facts per serving: 371 cal., 16 g total fat (9 g sat. fat), 60 mg chol., 1,326 mg sodium, 33 g carbo. (6 g sugar), 2 g fiber, 24 g pro.
Exchanges: 2 Starch, 2½ Medium-Fat Meat, ½ Fat

get active

Shoveling snow doesn't have to be all hard work. Shovel it into a pile and then build a fort or a snow person.

NACHO CHEESE CHICKEN CHOWDER

PREP: 10 minutes **COOK:** Low 4 hours, High 2 hours **MAKES:** 6 servings

1 **pound skinless, boneless chicken breast halves, cut into ½-inch pieces**

2 **14½-ounce cans Mexican-style stewed tomatoes, undrained**

1 **10¾-ounce can condensed nacho cheese soup**

1 **10-ounce package frozen whole kernel corn (2 cups)**

Packaged baked tortilla chips and/or Easy Fresh Salsa (see recipe, page 121) or bottled salsa (optional)

ONE In a 3½- or 4-quart slow cooker stir together chicken, undrained tomatoes, soup, and corn.

TWO Cover and cook on low-heat setting for 4 to 5 hours or on high-heat setting for 2 to 2½ hours. Ladle soup into bowls. If desired, sprinkle with tortilla chips and/or salsa.

Nutrition Facts per serving: 221 cal., 5 g total fat (2 g sat. fat), 50 mg chol., 835 mg sodium, 23 g carbo. (2 g sugar), 2 g fiber, 22 g pro.
Exchanges: 1 Vegetable, 1 Starch, 2½ Very Lean Meat, ½ Fat

QUICK TOMATO SOUP

START TO FINISH: 20 minutes **MAKES:** 4 or 5 servings

- **3 tablespoons butter**
- **3 tablespoons all-purpose flour**
- **1 14-ounce can chicken broth**
- **½ cup milk**
- **2½ cups vegetable juice or tomato juice**
- **1 teaspoon dried basil or Italian seasoning, crushed**
- **¼ teaspoon salt**
- **¼ teaspoon black pepper**

ONE In a medium saucepan melt butter. Stir in flour; cook and stir over medium heat for 1 minute. Add broth and milk all at once. Cook and stir until mixture is slightly thickened and bubbly. Cook and stir for 1 minute more.

TWO Stir in vegetable juice, basil, salt, and pepper. Simmer gently, uncovered, for 5 minutes more, stirring occasionally. Serve immediately.

Nutrition Facts per serving: 152 cal., 10 g total fat (5 g sat. fat), 28 mg chol., 1,038 mg sodium, 13 g carbo. (7 g sugar), 1 g fiber, 4 g pro.
Exchanges: 1 Vegetable, ½ Other Carbo., 2 Fat

cut the sugar

Many store-bought tomato soups are packed with unneeded sugar—almost double the amount in this Quick Tomato Soup recipe.

TATER SOUP

START TO FINISH: 40 minutes MAKES: 4 to 6 servings

4   medium round red, white,
    or yellow potatoes, cut
    into bite-size pieces
    (about 1¼ pounds)

½   cup sliced carrot

½   cup sliced celery

2   tablespoons butter
    or margarine

2   tablespoons all-purpose
    flour

½   teaspoon salt

⅛   teaspoon white pepper

1½ cups milk

1   14-ounce can reduced-
    sodium chicken broth

    Shredded reduced-fat
    cheddar cheese
    (optional)

ONE In a large saucepan cook unpeeled potatoes in a large amount of boiling salted water for 5 minutes. Add carrot and celery. Cook, covered, about 10 minutes more or until vegetables are tender; drain. Transfer 1 cup of the vegetable mixture to a small bowl; transfer remaining vegetable mixture to another bowl and set aside. Use a potato masher to mash the 1 cup vegetables until nearly smooth. Set mashed vegetable mixture aside.

TWO In same saucepan melt butter. Stir in flour, salt, and white pepper. Add milk all at once. Cook and stir until slightly thickened and bubbly. Cook and stir for 2 minutes more.

THREE Stir in reserved cooked vegetables, mashed vegetable mixture, and broth. Cook and stir over medium heat until heated through. If necessary, stir in additional milk to reach desired consistency. Season to taste with additional salt and white pepper. If desired, sprinkle with shredded cheese.

Nutrition Facts per serving: 234 cal., 8 g total fat (5 g sat. fat), 24 mg chol., 698 mg sodium, 33 g carbo. (8 g sugar), 3 g fiber, 8 g pro.
Exchanges: ½ Milk, ½ Vegetable, 1½ Starch, 1 Fat

get active

Lace up your skates and head to the rink. Even if you're just learning to skate, you'll still get a workout.

TACO SALAD BOWLS

PREP: 35 minutes **BAKE:** 10 minutes **OVEN:** 350°F **MAKES:** 4 servings

4 **6- to 8-inch whole wheat or plain flour tortillas**

   Nonstick cooking spray

12 **ounces lean ground beef or uncooked ground turkey**

1 **medium onion, chopped**

1 **clove garlic, minced**

1 **8-ounce can tomato sauce**

1 **tablespoon cider vinegar**

½ **teaspoon ground cumin**

¼ **teaspoon crushed red pepper**

4 **cups shredded lettuce**

¼ **cup shredded reduced-fat cheddar cheese (1 ounce)**

¼ **cup chopped green or red sweet pepper (optional)**

12 **cherry tomatoes, quartered**

ONE For tortilla bowls, wrap tortillas in foil. Warm in a 350° oven for 10 minutes. Coat four 10-ounce custard cups with nonstick cooking spray. Carefully press 1 tortilla into each cup. Bake in the 350° oven for 10 to 15 minutes or until golden and crisp. Cool; remove from custard cups.

TWO Meanwhile, in a large skillet cook beef, onion, and garlic until beef is brown and onion is tender. Drain fat.

THREE Stir tomato sauce, vinegar, cumin, and crushed red pepper into skillet. Bring to boiling; reduce heat. Simmer, uncovered, for 10 minutes.

FOUR Place tortillas on 4 serving plates. Spoon beef mixture into tortillas. Sprinkle with lettuce, cheese, sweet pepper, if desired, and tomatoes.

MAKE-AHEAD: Prepare tortilla bowls. Place in large freezer container with paper towels between bowls and crumpled around sides to protect the shells. Seal, label, and freeze for up to 1 month.

Nutrition Facts per serving: 297 cal., 13 g total fat (4 g sat. fat), 59 mg chol., 575 mg sodium, 23 g carbo. (4 g sugar), 3 g fiber, 22 g pro.
Exchanges: 1½ Vegetable, 1 Starch, 2 Lean Meat, 1½ Fat

SUPER-CRUNCHY SUPPER SALAD

START TO FINISH: 35 minutes **MAKES:** 4 to 6 servings

3 **tablespoons apple juice**

3 **tablespoons salad oil**

1 **tablespoon red or white wine vinegar or cider vinegar**

4 **to 6 cups packaged mixed salad greens**

2 **medium apples or pears, cored and cut into wedges**

8 **ounces lean cooked beef, ham, chicken, or turkey, cut into thin bite-size strips (1½ cups)**

2 **medium carrots, cut into thin bite-size strips**

1 **cup zucchini, cucumber, or jicama cut into bite-size strips**

¼ **cup dried cherries or cranberries (optional)**

ONE For dressing, in a screw-top jar combine apple juice, oil, and vinegar. Cover and shake well.

TWO Divide greens among 4 to 6 dinner plates. Arrange apples, beef, carrots, zucchini, and, if desired, cherries on top of lettuce. Drizzle dressing over salads.

Nutrition Facts per serving: 249 cal., 13 g total fat (3 g sat. fat), 39 mg chol., 65 mg sodium, 16 g carbo. (11 g sugar), 3 g fiber, 18 g pro.
Exchanges: 1½ Vegetable, ½ Fruit, 2 Lean Meat, 1½ Fat

cut the sugar

Purchased salad dressings can have added sugars that aren't necessary. Homemade salad dressings are easy to make and you can control the ingredients.

STEAK SALAD WITH **BUTTERMILK** DRESSING

START TO FINISH: 30 minutes **MAKES:** 4 servings

6 **cups packaged mixed salad greens**

2 **medium carrots, cut into thin bite-size strips**

1 **medium yellow sweet pepper, cut into thin bite-size strips**

1 **cup cherry or pear-shaped tomatoes, halved**

8 **ounces boneless beef top sirloin steak**

Nonstick cooking spray

¼ **cup finely shredded fresh basil**

Salt and black pepper (optional)

1 **recipe Buttermilk Dressing**

Additional tomatoes (optional)

ONE Arrange salad greens, carrots, sweet pepper, and tomatoes on 4 dinner plates. Set aside. Trim fat from meat. Cut meat across the grain into thin bite-size strips.

TWO Lightly coat a large skillet with cooking spray. Heat over medium-high heat. Add meat. Cook and stir for 2 to 3 minutes or until meat is slightly pink in the center. Remove from heat. Stir in basil. If desired, lightly sprinkle with salt and black pepper.

THREE To serve, spoon warm meat mixture over greens mixture. Drizzle with Buttermilk Dressing. If desired, garnish with additional tomatoes. Serve immediately.

BUTTERMILK DRESSING: In a small bowl combine ½ cup low-fat plain yogurt; ⅓ cup buttermilk; 3 tablespoons freshly grated Parmesan cheese; 3 tablespoons finely chopped red onion; 3 tablespoons light mayonnaise or salad dressing; 2 tablespoons snipped fresh parsley; 1 tablespoon white wine vinegar or lemon juice; 1 clove garlic, minced; ¼ teaspoon salt; and ⅛ teaspoon black pepper. Cover and chill at least 30 minutes or until ready to serve.

Nutrition Facts per serving: 198 cal., 8 g total fat (3 g sat. fat), 44 mg chol., 374 mg sodium, 15 g carbo. (10 g sugar), 3 g fiber, 18 g pro.
Exchanges: 2 Vegetable, ½ Other Carbo., 2 Lean Meat

COOL-AS-A-CUCUMBER CHICKEN SALAD

START TO FINISH: 25 minutes **MAKES:** 4 to 6 servings

2 **cups shredded cooked chicken**

2 **cups peeled, seeded, and cubed cantaloupe and/or halved seedless red grapes**

1 **cup chopped cucumber**

$\frac{1}{3}$ **cup orange juice**

3 **tablespoons salad oil**

1 **tablespoon snipped fresh mint or cilantro**

Salt and black pepper

4 **cups shredded romaine lettuce or leaf lettuce**

ONE In a large bowl toss together chicken, cantaloupe and/or grapes, and cucumber.

TWO For dressing, in a screw-top jar combine orange juice, oil, and mint. Cover and shake well. Season to taste with salt and pepper. Drizzle over chicken mixture; toss lightly to coat.

THREE Divide lettuce among 4 dinner plates. Top with chicken mixture. Serve immediately.

TIP: For 2 cups shredded cooked chicken, purchase a deli-roasted chicken. Using 2 forks, shred enough of the chicken to make 2 cups, discarding the skin. Or use a 9-ounce package frozen chopped, cooked chicken, thawed. If you have more time, cook 12 ounces skinless, boneless chicken breast halves, covered, in $1\frac{1}{2}$ cups water about 15 minutes or until no longer pink (170°F). Drain well, cool slightly, and shred.

Nutrition Facts per serving: 269 cal., 16 g total fat (3 g sat. fat), 62 mg chol., 114 mg sodium, 11 g carbo. (9 g sugar), 1 g fiber, 22 g pro.
Exchanges: 1 Vegetable, $\frac{1}{2}$ Fruit, 3 Lean Meat, 1 Fat

SOUTHWESTERN CHICKEN
AND BLACK BEAN SALAD

START TO FINISH: 25 minutes **MAKES:** 6 to 8 servings

- **6 cups torn romaine lettuce or packaged mixed salad greens**
- **1 15-ounce can black beans, rinsed and drained**
- **1½ cups chopped cooked chicken or turkey (about 8 ounces)**
- **1½ cups red and/or yellow cherry tomatoes, halved**
- **⅓ cup reduced-calorie bottled Caesar or ranch salad dressing**
- **2 teaspoons chili powder**
- **½ teaspoon ground cumin**
- **2 tablespoons snipped fresh cilantro or parsley**
- **½ cup coarsely crushed purchased baked tortilla chips**

ONE In a large bowl combine lettuce, black beans, chicken, and tomatoes.

TWO For dressing, in a small bowl whisk together salad dressing, chili powder, and cumin. Pour dressing over salad. Toss lightly to coat. Sprinkle with cilantro and tortilla chips. Serve immediately.

TIP: To make your own baked tortilla chips, cut flour tortillas into 8 wedges each. Spread wedges in a 15X10X1-inch baking pan. Bake in a 375°F oven for 10 to 15 minutes or until dry and crisp, gently tossing once. Cool completely.

Nutrition Facts per serving: 178 cal., 5 g total fat (1 g sat. fat), 33 mg chol., 480 mg sodium, 17 g carbo. (2 g sugar), 6 g fiber, 16 g pro.
Exchanges: 1 Vegetable, 1 Starch, 1½ Very Lean Meat, ½ Fat

TERIYAKI CHICKEN NOODLE SALAD

START TO FINISH: 30 minutes **MAKES:** 8 to 10 servings

- **1 3-ounce package chicken- or Oriental-flavored ramen noodles**
- **¼ cup rice vinegar or white wine vinegar**
- **2 tablespoons orange juice**
- **2 tablespoons salad oil**
  Few dashes bottled hot pepper sauce (optional)
- **6 cups packaged mixed salad greens**
- **2 cups fresh vegetables, such as sliced carrots, yellow summer squash, zucchini, cucumber, and/or halved pea pods**
- **2 oranges, peeled, halved, and thinly sliced**
- **12 ounces skinless, boneless chicken breast halves**
- **2 tablespoons cooking oil**
  Coarsely ground black pepper (optional)

ONE For dressing, in a screw-top jar combine flavor packet from ramen noodles, vinegar, orange juice, salad oil, and, if desired, hot pepper sauce. Cover and shake well; set aside.

TWO In a large salad bowl combine salad greens, desired vegetables, and orange slices; toss gently to mix. Break ramen noodles into small pieces; add to salad. Cover and chill up to 1 hour.

THREE Meanwhile, cut chicken into thin bite-size strips. Pour cooking oil into a wok or large skillet. Heat over medium-high heat. Cook chicken in hot oil for 2 to 3 minutes or until no longer pink; drain off fat.

FOUR While chicken is cooking, pour dressing over salad mixture; toss gently to coat. Let stand about 10 minutes to soften noodles, tossing occasionally.

FIVE Add chicken to salad; toss gently. If desired, sprinkle with pepper. Serve immediately.

Nutrition Facts per serving: 188 cal., 10 g total fat (1 g sat. fat), 25 mg chol., 227 mg sodium, 12 g carbo. (4 g sugar), 1 g fiber, 12 g pro.
Exchanges: 1 Vegetable, ½ Starch, 1½ Very Lean Meat, 1½ Fat

SMOKED TURKEY AND TORTELLINI SALAD

START TO FINISH: 25 minutes **MAKES:** 4 servings

1 **7- to 8-ounce package dried cheese-filled tortellini**

1 **cup chopped, cooked smoked turkey, ham, or chicken**

8 **cherry tomatoes, quartered**

½ **cup coarsely chopped green sweet pepper**

¼ **cup sliced pitted ripe olives (optional)**

¼ **cup bottled Italian vinaigrette or balsamic vinaigrette salad dressing**

Black pepper

ONE Cook tortellini according to package directions; drain. Rinse with cold water; drain again.

TWO In a large bowl combine tortellini, turkey, tomatoes, sweet pepper, and, if desired, olives. Drizzle salad dressing over mixture; toss to coat. Season to taste with black pepper. Serve immediately.

TIP: For a vegetarian salad, replace the turkey with 1 cup chopped raw broccoli or cauliflower.

Nutrition Facts per serving: 330 cal., 15 g total fat (2 g sat. fat), 20 mg chol., 897 mg sodium, 32 g carbo. (2 g sugar), 1 g fiber, 17 g pro.
Exchanges: ½ Vegetable, 1½ Starch, ½ Other Carbo., 2 Very Lean Meat, 2 Fat

CHEF SALAD

START TO FINISH: 30 minutes **MAKES:** 4 servings

6 cups packaged torn mixed salad greens

4 ounces cooked lower-fat ham or turkey, cut into bite-size pieces

½ cup shredded reduced-fat cheddar cheese (2 ounces)

1 hard-cooked egg, sliced

8 cherry tomatoes, halved

1 small yellow or red sweet pepper, cut into bite-size strips

½ cup purchased croutons

½ cup bottled reduced-calorie ranch salad dressing

ONE Divide greens among 4 large salad plates. Arrange ham, cheese, egg, tomatoes, and sweet pepper on top of the greens. Sprinkle with croutons. Drizzle with dressing.

TIP: For a decorative touch, use tiny cookie or hors d'oeuvre cutters to cut the sweet pepper into shapes.

Nutrition Facts per serving: 191 cal., 11 g total fat (2 g sat. fat), 85 mg chol., 783 mg sodium, 11 g carbo. (3 g sugar), 2 g fiber, 12 g pro. **Exchanges:** 2 Vegetable, 1 Lean Meat, 2 Fat

TURKEY AND PASTA SALAD

START TO FINISH: 30 minutes **MAKES:** 6 to 8 servings

- **6 ounces dried radiatore or rotelle pasta**
- **1 medium apple, cored and chopped**
- **1 tablespoon lime or lemon juice**
- **8 ounces smoked turkey breast, cut into bite-size pieces**
- **1 cup quartered fresh strawberries**
- **1/2 cup sliced celery**
- **1/4 cup low-fat plain yogurt**
- **2 tablespoons light mayonnaise or salad dressing**
- **2 tablespoons fat-free milk**
- **1 to 2 tablespoons Dijon-style mustard**
- **1/8 teaspoon salt**
- **1 tablespoon snipped fresh basil (optional)**

ONE Cook pasta according to package directions; drain. Rinse with cold water and drain again. Toss chopped apple with lime juice to coat. In a large bowl combine drained pasta, apple, turkey, strawberries, and celery.

TWO For dressing, in a small bowl combine yogurt, mayonnaise, milk, mustard, and salt. Drizzle dressing over pasta mixture; toss gently to coat. If desired, sprinkle with basil.

Nutrition Facts per serving: 191 cal., 3 g total fat (1 g sat. fat), 19 mg chol., 537 mg sodium, 29 g carbo. (6 g sugar), 2 g fiber, 13 g pro.
Exchanges: 1½ Starch, ½ Other Carbo., 1½ Very Lean Meat

cut the sugar

Apple chunks give this Turkey and Pasta Salad a naturally sweet taste without adding sugar. For a twist, try grapes instead of apples.

wrap &

roll

Whether for a brown-bag lunch or super-quick dinner, sandwiches are the solution for busy families. These range from warm barbecue beef to cool ranch wraps. We've added fruits and vegetables to most of these sandwiches, making it easier to get in your daily dose of nutrients.

BARBECUE BEEF SANDWICHES

PREP: 30 minutes **COOK:** 1½ hours **MAKES:** 8 sandwiches

1 **2-pound beef round steak, cut ¾ inch thick**

Nonstick cooking spray

1 **14½-ounce can diced tomatoes, undrained**

1 **large onion, chopped (1 cup)**

1 **large carrot, chopped (¾ cup)**

1 **clove garlic, minced**

2 **tablespoons Worcestershire sauce**

2 **tablespoons vinegar**

2 **teaspoons chili powder**

1 **teaspoon dried oregano, crushed**

¼ **teaspoon salt**

Salt and black pepper

8 **whole wheat hamburger buns**

ONE Trim fat from meat. Cut meat into 4 to 6 pieces. Coat a Dutch oven with nonstick cooking spray. Brown meat, half at a time, in Dutch oven over medium heat, turning to brown both sides. Return all meat to Duch oven.

TWO Add undrained tomatoes, onion, carrot, garlic, Worcestershire sauce, vinegar, chili powder, oregano, and ¼ teaspoon salt. Bring to boiling; reduce heat. Simmer, covered, for 1½ to 2 hours or until meat is very tender.

THREE Remove meat from sauce. Use 2 forks to shred meat. Return shredded meat to sauce; heat through. Season to taste with additional salt and pepper. Divide meat mixture among buns.

MAKE-AHEAD: Transfer meat and sauce to 1-, 2-, or 4-serving-size freezer containers. Cover, label, and freeze for up to 6 months. To reheat, transfer mixture to a saucepan; add 1 tablespoon water. Cook over low heat until heated through, stirring occasionally. Allow 8 to 10 minutes for 1 or 2 servings; 25 to 30 minutes for 4 servings. Serve on buns.

Nutrition Facts per sandwich: 304 cal., 7 g total fat (2 g sat. fat), 65 mg chol., 511 mg sodium, 29 g carbo. (7 g sugar), 2 g fiber, 29 g pro.
Exchanges: ½ Vegetable, 2 Starch, 3 Lean Meat

BURGERS WITH A TWIST

START TO FINISH: 25 minutes **MAKES:** 8 servings

1½   **pounds lean ground beef**

½   **cup chopped onion (1 medium)**

⅓   **cup chopped green sweet pepper**

1   **10¾-ounce can reduced-fat and reduced-sodium condensed tomato soup**

1   **tablespoon Worcestershire sauce**

1   **tablespoon prepared mustard**

   Dill pickle slices (optional)

8   **whole wheat or white hamburger buns, split and toasted**

ONE In a large skillet cook ground beef, onion, and sweet pepper until beef is brown. Drain off fat. Stir in soup, Worcestershire sauce, and mustard. Bring to boiling; reduce heat. Simmer, covered, for 5 minutes. If desired, serve with pickles on toasted hamburger buns.

Nutrition Facts per serving: 289 cal., 11 g total fat (4 g sat. fat), 54 mg chol., 417 mg sodium, 27 g carbo. (4 g sugar), 2 g fiber, 20 g pro.
Exchanges: 2 Starch, 2 Medium-Fat Meat

ITALIAN-STYLE SLOPPY JOES

PREP: 30 minutes **BAKE:** 20 minutes **OVEN:** 400°F **MAKES:** 8 servings

12 **ounces lean ground beef**

1 **8-ounce can tomato sauce**

1 **tablespoon dried minced onion**

¼ **teaspoon dried oregano, crushed**

¼ **teaspoon dried basil, crushed**

8 **3-inch hard rolls**

1 **cup shredded mozzarella cheese (4 ounces)**

¼ **cup grated Parmesan cheese**

Carrot sticks (optional)

ONE In a large skillet cook ground beef until brown. Drain off fat. Stir in tomato sauce, onion, oregano, and basil. Bring mixture to boiling; reduce heat. Simmer, covered, for 15 minutes.

TWO Meanwhile, cut a thin slice from the top of each roll; set tops of rolls aside. Scoop out insides of rolls, leaving ½-inch-thick shells. Set shells aside. Reserve scooped-out bread for another use.

THREE Spoon beef mixture evenly into bread shells. Top with mozzarella and Parmesan cheeses. Cover with roll tops. Wrap each roll in foil. Place on a large baking sheet. Bake in a 400° oven about 20 minutes or until heated through. If desired, serve with carrot sticks.

Nutrition Facts per serving: 291 cal., 9 g total fat (4 g sat. fat), 38 mg chol., 580 mg sodium, 32 g carbo. (2 g sugar), 2 g fiber, 18 g pro.
Exchanges: 2 Starch, 2 Lean Meat, ½ Fat

MEATBALL PITAS

PREP: 25 minutes **BAKE:** 20 minutes **OVEN:** 350°F **MAKES:** 8 servings

get active

Sing a song while jumping rope. Speed it up or down depending on how fast you jump.

½ cup low-fat plain yogurt

1 teaspoon lemon juice

1 clove garlic, minced

¼ teaspoon salt

12 ounces lean ground beef

1 tablespoon snipped fresh oregano or 1 teaspoon dried oregano, crushed

¾ teaspoon salt

1 clove garlic, minced

⅛ to ¼ teaspoon cayenne pepper

4 large whole wheat pita bread rounds, halved crosswise

8 lettuce leaves

Tomato wedges (optional)

ONE For sauce, in a small bowl combine yogurt, lemon juice, 1 clove garlic, and ¼ teaspoon salt. Set aside.

TWO For meatballs, in a medium bowl combine ground beef, oregano, ¾ teaspoon salt, 1 clove garlic, and cayenne pepper; mix well. Form beef mixture into 24 meatballs about 1 inch in diameter. Place meatballs in a 15X10X1-inch baking pan.

THREE Bake meatballs, uncovered, in a 350° oven about 20 minutes or until no longer pink.

FOUR Carefully open pita bread halves. Line each half with a lettuce leaf. Fill each half with 3 meatballs, 1 tablespoon sauce, and (if desired) tomato wedges.

Nutrition Facts per serving: 168 cal., 5 g total fat (2 g sat. fat), 28 mg chol., 489 mg sodium, 19 g carbo. (2 g sugar), 2 g fiber, 12 g pro.
Exchanges: ½ Vegetable, 1 Starch, 1 Lean Meat, ½ Fat

FAJITA-RANCH CHICKEN WRAPS

START TO FINISH: 20 minutes **MAKES:** 4 servings

12 ounces skinless, boneless chicken breast strips for stir-frying

$\frac{1}{2}$ teaspoon chili powder

$\frac{1}{4}$ teaspoon garlic powder

Nonstick cooking spray

1 small red, yellow, or green sweet pepper, seeded and cut into thin strips

2 tablespoons bottled reduced-calorie ranch salad dressing

2 10-inch whole wheat, tomato, jalapeño, or plain flour tortillas, warmed

$\frac{1}{2}$ cup Easy Fresh Salsa (see recipe, page 121)

$\frac{1}{3}$ cup reduced-fat shredded cheddar cheese

ONE Sprinkle chicken strips with chili powder and garlic powder. Coat a medium nonstick skillet with nonstick spray; heat over medium-high heat. Cook chicken and sweet pepper strips in hot skillet over medium heat for 4 to 6 minutes or until chicken is no longer pink and pepper strips are tender. Drain if necessary. Toss with salad dressing.

TWO Divide chicken and pepper mixture between warmed tortillas. Top with Easy Fresh Salsa and cheese. Roll up; cut in half.

TO WARM TORTILLAS: Wrap tortillas tightly in foil. Heat in a 350°F oven about 10 minutes or until heated through.

Nutrition Facts per serving: 224 cal., 7 g total fat (2 g sat. fat), 59 mg chol., 316 mg sodium, 15 g carbo. (2 g sugar), 1 g fiber, 25 g pro.
Exchanges: 1 Starch, 3 Very Lean Meat, 1 Fat

PULLED CHICKEN SANDWICHES

START TO FINISH: 25 minutes **MAKES:** 6 sandwiches

1 **recipe Barbecue Sauce**

2 **cups shredded cooked chicken**

6 **whole wheat hamburger buns, split**

Red onion slices (optional)

Dill pickle spears (optional)

ONE Prepare Barbecue Sauce. Add shredded chicken to sauce. Heat through, stirring frequently. Serve on split buns. If desired, serve with red onion slices and dill pickle spears.

BARBECUE SAUCE: In a medium saucepan heat 1 tablespoon olive oil over medium heat. Add ¼ cup finely chopped onion; cook for 3 to 5 minutes or until tender, stirring occasionally. Add one 8-ounce can tomato sauce, 2 tablespoons tomato paste, 1 tablespoon Dijon-style mustard, 1 tablespoon Worcestershire sauce, and 1 teaspoon honey or heat-stable granular sugar substitute (Splenda). Bring to boiling; reduce heat. Simmer, uncovered, about 5 minutes or until sauce is desired consistency. Season to taste with salt and black pepper.

TIP: For shredded chicken, use a purchased roasted chicken. Pull the meat from the chicken, discarding skin and bones. Use 2 forks to pull chicken into shreds.

Nutrition Facts per sandwich: 254 cal., 8 g total fat (2 g sat. fat), 42 mg chol., 539 mg sodium, 27 g carbo. (5 g sugar), 1 g fiber, 19 g pro.
Exchanges: 2 Starch, 2 Lean Meat

get active

Use your backyard to host tournaments for basketball, softball, volleyball, kick ball, and dodgeball.

THAI **CHICKEN-BROCCOLI** WRAPS photo, p. 84-85

START TO FINISH: 25 minutes   **MAKES:** 6 servings

12 **ounces skinless, boneless chicken breast strips for stir-frying**

¼ **teaspoon garlic salt**

⅛ **teaspoon black pepper**

   Nonstick cooking spray

2 **cups packaged shredded broccoli (broccoli slaw mix)**

¼ **teaspoon ground ginger**

3 **10-inch whole wheat or plain flour tortillas, warmed**

1 **recipe Peanut Sauce**

ONE Sprinkle chicken strips with garlic salt and pepper. Coat a large nonstick skillet with nonstick cooking spray. Cook and stir seasoned chicken in hot skillet over medium-high heat for 2 to 3 minutes or until chicken is no longer pink. Remove chicken from skillet; keep warm. Add broccoli and ginger to skillet. Cook and stir for 2 to 3 minutes or until vegetables are crisp-tender.

TWO To assemble wraps, spread tortillas with Peanut Sauce. Top with chicken strips and vegetable mixture. Roll up each tortilla, securing with a toothpick. Cut in half. Serve immediately.

PEANUT SAUCE: In a small saucepan combine 3 tablespoons creamy peanut butter, 2 tablespoons water, 1 tablespoon reduced-sodium soy sauce, ½ teaspoon bottled minced garlic, and ¼ teaspoon ground ginger. Heat over very low heat until smooth, whisking constantly.

TO WARM TORTILLAS: Wrap tortillas tightly in foil. Heat in a 350°F oven about 10 minutes or until heated through.

Nutrition Facts per serving: 191 cal., 6 g total fat (1 g sat. fat), 33 mg chol., 460 mg sodium, 16 g carbo. (3 g sugar), 2 g fiber, 18 g pro.
Exchanges: ½ Vegetable, 1 Starch, 2 Very Lean Meat, ½ Fat

cut the sugar

Watch out when using purchased peanut sauce with Thai foods. One tiny serving packs 5 grams of sugar.

CHICKEN AND HUMMUS PITAS

PREP: 20 minutes **BROIL:** 12 minutes **MAKES:** 4 servings

- 1 **tablespoon olive oil**
- 1 **teaspoon lemon juice**
- ¼ **teaspoon paprika**
- **Dash salt**
- **Dash black pepper**
- 2 **skinless, boneless chicken breast halves (8 to 12 ounces)**
- 2 **large whole wheat pita bread rounds, halved crosswise**
- 1 **7-ounce carton hummus**
- ¾ **cup coarsely chopped roma tomatoes**
- ½ **cup thinly sliced cucumber**
- ⅓ **cup plain low-fat yogurt**

ONE In a small bowl combine oil, lemon juice, paprika, salt, and pepper. Place chicken on the unheated rack of a broiler pan. Brush both sides of chicken with the oil mixture. Broil 4 to 5 inches from heat for 7 minutes. Turn chicken; broil 5 to 8 minutes more or until chicken is no longer pink. Cool slightly; cut into strips.

TWO To serve, carefully open pita halves and spead hummus inside; stuff with chicken, tomatoes, cucumber, and yogurt.

Nutrition Facts per serving: 289 cal., 10 g total fat (2 g sat. fat), 34 mg chol., 380 mg sodium, 31 g carbo. (3 g sugar), 5 g fiber, 20 g pro.
Exchanges: 1½ Starch, ½ Other Carbo., 2 Very Lean Meat, 1 Fat

cut the sugar

Grilling veggies brings out their natural sweetness, making these Grilled Veggie Wraps naturally sweet without added sugar.

GRILLED VEGGIE WRAPS

PREP: 30 minutes **GRILL:** 8 minutes **MAKES:** 6 servings

- **1 large red or green sweet pepper, seeded and cut into ½-inch strips**
- **1 medium yellow summer squash, cut lengthwise into ¼-inch slices**
- **1 small sweet red onion, cut into 1-inch wedges**
- **2 teaspoons cooking oil**
- **3 12-inch tomato and/or spinach flour tortillas, grilled, if desired**
- **3 tablespoons bottled reduced-calorie ranch salad dressing**
- **4 ounces thinly sliced, cooked turkey breast**
- **2 ounces Monterey Jack cheese with jalapeño peppers or Monterey Jack cheese, cut into thin slices**
- **¼ cup snipped fresh cilantro**

ONE Brush sweet pepper, squash, and onion with oil. Grill sweet pepper in a grill wok, grill basket, or on a greased grilling tray on an uncovered grill directly over medium-hot coals for 3 minutes.

TWO Add squash and onion to grill. Grill vegetables for 5 to 8 minutes more or until crisp-tender, turning occasionally. Remove vegetables from grill as they are done; set aside and keep warm. If desired, warm tortillas on the grill for 1 to 2 minutes.

THREE To assemble wraps, spread 1 side of each tortilla with ranch dressing. Arrange turkey on top of dressing. Top with slices of cheese. Spoon one-third of the grilled vegetables over cheese just below center of each tortilla. Top vegetables with snipped cilantro. Fold bottom third of tortillas partially over the vegetables. Fold in sides. Roll tortilla up tightly. Cut wraps into thirds.

Nutrition Facts per serving: 221 cal., 9 g total fat (2 g sat. fat), 25 mg chol., 482 mg sodium, 24 g carbo. (2 g sugar), 1 g fiber, 12 g pro.
Exchanges: 1 Vegetable, 1 Starch, 1 Very Lean Meat, 1½ Fat

get active

Play a "hot potato" game of flying discs with friends and family. You'll move faster than you do with the regular tossing game and get a better workout.

HOT APPLE AND CHEESE SANDWICHES

START TO FINISH: 25 minutes **MAKES:** 4 servings

1 medium apple or pear

4 whole wheat English muffins, split

2 tablespoons Dijon-style mustard

4 slices Canadian-style bacon

4 slices Swiss cheese

Apple chunks (optional)

ONE Core apple and thinly slice crosswise to form rings. Spread cut sides of muffin halves with mustard.

TWO To assemble, top 4 of the muffin halves with a slice of bacon, 1 or 2 apple rings, and a slice of cheese. Top with remaining muffin halves, cut sides down.

THREE Heat a large nonstick skillet or griddle. Place sandwiches in skillet or on griddle. Cook over medium-low heat for 9 to 10 minutes or until sandwiches are golden brown and cheese starts to melt, turning once. If desired, garnish sandwiches with apple chunks.

Nutrition Facts per serving: 303 cal., 11 g total fat (6 g sat. fat), 40 mg chol., 851 mg sodium, 34 g carbo. (5 g sugar), 3 g fiber, 20 g pro.
Exchanges: 2 Starch, 2 Medium-Fat Meat

HAM AND CHEESE CALZONES

PREP: 15 minutes **BAKE:** 15 minutes **STAND:** 5 minutes **OVEN:** 400°F **MAKES:** 4 servings

1 10-ounce package refrigerated pizza dough

¼ cup Dijon-style mustard

4 ounces sliced Swiss or provolone cheese

8 ounces low-fat thinly sliced cooked ham, chopped (1½ cups)

Milk (optional)

ONE Line a baking sheet with foil; lightly grease foil. Unroll pizza dough. On a lightly floured surface, roll or pat dough into a 15X10-inch rectangle. Cut dough in half crosswise and lengthwise to make 4 rectangles. Spread mustard over rectangles. Divide half of the cheese among rectangles, placing cheese on half of each and cutting or tearing to fit as necessary. Top with ham. Top with remaining cheese. Brush edges with water. Fold dough over filling to opposite edge, stretching slightly if necessary. Use the tines of a fork to press edges to seal.

TWO Place calzones on prepared baking sheet. Prick tops to allow steam to escape. If desired, brush tops with milk. Bake in a 400° oven about 15 minutes or until golden brown. Let stand for 5 minutes before serving.

Nutrition Facts per serving: 334 cal., 12 g total fat (6 g sat. fat), 53 mg chol., 1131 mg sodium, 33 g carbo. (2 g sugar), 1 g fiber, 24 g pro.
Exchanges: 2 Starch, 2½ Medium-Fat Meat

CHEESY GRILLED HAM SANDWICHES

START TO FINISH: 15 minutes **MAKES:** 2 servings

2 to 3 teaspoons Dijon-style mustard

4 slices firm wheat bread, white bread, or sourdough bread

2 ounces thinly sliced cooked ham

2 slices Swiss cheese (2 ounces)

¼ cup fat-free milk

1 egg white

   Nonstick cooking spray

ONE Spread mustard on 2 of the bread slices. Top with ham and cheese. Place remaining bread slices on top of ham and cheese. In a shallow bowl or pie plate beat together milk and egg white.

TWO Coat an unheated nonstick griddle or large skillet with nonstick cooking spray. Heat over medium heat. Dip each sandwich in milk mixture, turning to coat. Place on griddle or in skillet; cook for 1 to 2 minutes on each side or until golden and cheese melts.

Nutrition Facts per serving: 317 cal., 13 g total fat (6 g sat. fat), 43 mg chol., 855 mg sodium, 31 g carbo. (6 g sugar), 0 g fiber, 20 g pro.
Exchanges: 2 Starch, 2 Lean Meat, 1 Fat

cut the sugar

A similar sandwich—the Monte Cristo—is covered in powdered sugar. But this Cheesy Grilled Ham Sandwich is so full of flavor, it doesn't need the added sugar.

HEARTY TURKEY ROLL-UPS

PREP: 25 minutes **BAKE:** 25 minutes **STAND:** 10 minutes **OVEN:** 375°F **MAKES:** 6 servings

1 **13.8-ounce package refrigerated pizza dough**

4 **ounces thinly sliced cooked turkey**

1 **cup shredded mozzarella cheese (4 ounces)**

4 **ounces thinly sliced cooked turkey pepperoni**

⅓ **cup chopped yellow, red, or green sweet pepper**

Milk

Pizza or pasta sauce (optional)

ONE On a lightly floured surface, carefully roll pizza dough into a 13X10-inch rectangle. Layer turkey, half of the cheese, pepperoni, remaining cheese, and sweet pepper on dough to within ½ inch of edges. Starting from a long side, roll up into a spiral; pinch edge and ends to seal.

TWO Place loaf, seam side down, on a lightly greased baking sheet. Brush with milk. Using a sharp knife, make a few shallow cuts across top of loaf. Bake in a 375° oven for 25 minutes or until golden brown. Let stand for 10 minutes before slicing. If desired, serve with warm pizza sauce.

Nutrition Facts per serving: 270 cal., 9 g total fat (4 g sat. fat), 52 mg chol., 685 mg sodium, 26 g carbo. (1 g sugar), 1 g fiber, 20 g pro.
Exchanges: 2 Starch, 2 Lean Meat

HAM SPIRALS

PREP: 25 minutes **STAND:** per cracker bread package directions **MAKES:** 6 to 8 servings

- **1** **15-inch round Armenian cracker bread (lavosh)**
- **½** **of an 8-ounce package reduced-fat cream cheese (Neufchâtel), softened**
- **1** **tablespoon milk**
- **½** **cup finely chopped green, red, or yellow sweet pepper**
- **8** **ounces thinly sliced cooked ham**
- **6** **small butterhead (Boston or Bibb) lettuce leaves**

ONE Soften cracker bread according to package directions.

TWO Meanwhile, in a medium bowl stir together cream cheese and milk until smooth. Stir in sweet pepper.

THREE Spread cream cheese mixture onto softened cracker bread. Top with ham. Arrange lettuce leaves over half of the surface. Roll up tightly from lettuce-topped side. (If desired, wrap and chill up to 4 hours.) To serve, cut crosswise into 6 or 8 pieces.

TIP: For tortilla rolls, substitute four 8- to 10-inch whole wheat or plain flour tortillas for the cracker bread; do not soften. Spread tortillas with cream cheese mixture. Top with ham and lettuce. Roll up. Cut each roll into 3 or 4 pieces.

Nutrition Facts per serving: 213 cal., 9 g total fat (4 g sat. fat), 36 mg chol., 740 mg sodium, 21 g carbo. (1 g sugar), 1 g fiber, 11 g pro.
Exchanges: ½ Vegetable, 1 Starch, 1 Lean Meat, 1 Fat

TALL TURKEY SANDWICH

START TO FINISH: 5 minutes **MAKES:** 1 serving

1 tablespoon fat-free plain yogurt

2 teaspoons Dijon-style mustard

2 slices multi-grain bread, toasted

3 to 4 leaves lettuce, such as leaf or Bibb

2 to 3 ounces sliced cooked fat-free turkey breast

2 slices tomato

1 slice yellow sweet pepper

¼ cup snow pea pods, cut lengthwise into thin pieces (optional)

ONE In a small bowl stir together yogurt and mustard; spread mixture on 1 toasted bread slice. Layer lettuce, turkey, tomato, and sweet pepper on top of bread. Add the pea pods, if desired, and second toasted bread slice.

Nutrition Facts per serving: 225 cal., 2 g total fat (1 g sat. fat), 21 mg chol., 1,211 mg sodium, 34 g carbo. (7 g sugar), 4 g fiber, 17 g pro.
Exchanges: 1 Vegetable, 2 Starch, 1½ Very Lean Meat

get active

Rollerblade often, wearing a helmet, elbow pads, and knee pads. Each time you do, try to go farther and faster.

CHICKEN SALAD SANDWICHES

START TO FINISH: 20 minutes **MAKES:** 4 sandwiches

1   cup chopped cooked chicken

1/3 cup chopped cored apple,
    chopped seeded cucumber,
    or finely chopped celery

1   hard-cooked egg, peeled
    and chopped

2   tablespoons plain
    low-fat yogurt

2   tablespoons light mayonnaise
    or salad dressing
    Salt and black pepper

8   slices whole wheat bread

ONE In a medium bowl stir together chicken, apple, and egg. Add yogurt and mayonnaise; stir to combine. Season to taste with salt and pepper. Serve immediately or cover and chill up to 4 hours.

TWO Spread chicken mixture on half of the bread slices. Top with remaining bread slices. If desired, cut away crusts. Cut each sandwich into 4 triangles or squares.

Nutrition Facts per sandwich: 244 cal., 9 g total fat (2 g sat. fat), 87 mg chol., 432 mg sodium, 26 g carbo. (12 g sugar), 4 g fiber, 17 g pro.
Exchanges: 2 Starch, 1½ Lean Meat, ½ Fat

EGG AND VEGETABLE SALAD WRAPS

START TO FINISH: 30 minutes **MAKES:** 6 servings

- **2 hard-cooked eggs, chopped**
- **½ cup chopped cucumber**
- **½ cup chopped zucchini or yellow summer squash**
- **¼ cup chopped red onion**
- **¼ cup shredded carrot**
- **2 tablespoons fat-free or light mayonnaise or salad dressing**
- **1 tablespoon Dijon-style mustard**
- **2 teaspoons fat-free milk**
- **½ teaspoon snipped fresh basil**
- **Dash paprika**
- **3 leaves leaf lettuce**
- **3 10-inch spinach, vegetable, or plain flour tortillas**
- **1 roma tomato, thinly sliced**

ONE In a large bowl combine eggs, cucumber, zucchini, onion, and carrot. For dressing, in a small bowl stir together mayonnaise, mustard, milk, basil, and paprika. Pour dressing over egg mixture; toss gently to coat.

TWO For each wrap, place a lettuce leaf on a tortilla. Top with tomato slices, slightly off center. Spoon egg mixture on top of the tomato slices. Fold in 2 opposite sides of the tortilla; roll up from the bottom. Cut tortilla rolls in half diagonally.

Nutrition Facts per serving: 198 cal., 5 g total fat (1 g sat. fat), 71 mg chol., 412 mg sodium, 30 g carbo. (3 g sugar), 3 g fiber, 8 g pro.
Exchanges: ½ Vegetable, 1 Starch, ½ Other Carbo., ½ Lean Meat, 1 Fat

get active

When out shopping, park far from the store and race walk to the entrance.

restaurant

Kids both old and young love to go out to eat. But most restaurant fare is high in sugar, fat, and salt. You can create healthier versions of tacos, burritos, pizza, and nachos by using fresh fruits and veggies, fat-free beans, lean ground beef, and prepackaged bread dough. Most of these recipes can be whipped up in less than 30 minutes—now that's fast!

favorites

cut the sugar

Prepared spaghetti sauces have between 8 and 13 grams of sugar per serving. But Pasta with Just Tomatoes Sauce has less than 5 grams of sugar per serving.

PASTA WITH JUST TOMATOES SAUCE

START TO FINISH: 20 minutes **MAKES:** 6 servings

10 ounces dried pasta

1 14½-ounce can diced tomatoes, undrained

1 15-ounce can tomato sauce

2 tablespoons tomato paste

1 teaspoon dried Italian seasoning, crushed

Salt and black pepper

¼ cup grated Parmesan or Romano cheese

ONE Cook pasta according to package directions; drain.

TWO Meanwhile, in a medium saucepan combine undrained tomatoes, tomato sauce, tomato paste, and Italian seasoning. Cook over medium-low heat until heated through, stirring occasionally. Season to taste with salt and pepper.

THREE Divide pasta among 6 plates. Top each serving with tomato sauce. Sprinkle with cheese.

TIP: Add 1 cup of your favorite cooked vegetables to the sauce; heat through.

Nutrition Facts per serving: 230 cal., 2 g total fat (1 g sat. fat), 3 mg chol., 517 mg sodium, 43 g carbo. (5 g sugar), 2 g fiber, 9 g pro.
Exchanges: 1½ Vegetable, 2 Starch, ½ Other Carbo.

TASTES-LIKE-A-TACO PASTA SAUCE

- 8 ounces lean ground beef
- 1 large onion, chopped
- 1 medium green, red, or yellow sweet pepper, seeded and chopped
- 2 cloves garlic, minced
- 1 15-ounce can tomato sauce
- 1 14$\frac{1}{2}$-ounce can diced tomatoes, undrained
- 1$\frac{1}{2}$ teaspoons chili powder
- $\frac{1}{4}$ teaspoon ground cumin
  Salt and black pepper
- 10 ounces dried pasta
- 2 tablespoons snipped fresh cilantro
- $\frac{1}{2}$ cup shredded Monterey Jack or cheddar cheese

ONE In a large saucepan cook beef, onion, sweet pepper, and garlic over medium heat until beef is brown. Drain off fat. Stir in tomato sauce, undrained tomatoes, chili powder, and cumin. Bring to boiling; reduce heat. Simmer, uncovered, for 10 to 15 minutes or until desired consistency, stirring occasionally. Season to taste with salt and black pepper.

TWO Meanwhile, cook pasta according to package directions; drain. Just before serving, stir cilantro into sauce. Serve over hot cooked pasta. Sprinkle with cheese.

Nutrition Facts per serving: 325 cal., 7 g total fat (3 g sat. fat), 32 mg chol., 562 mg sodium, 47 g carbo. (6 g sugar), 3 g fiber, 17 g pro.
Exchanges: 1$\frac{1}{2}$ Vegetable, 2 Starch, $\frac{1}{2}$ Other Carbo., 1 Lean Meat, 1 Fat

PIZZA LOVER'S PASTA SAUCE

PREP: 25 minutes **COOK:** 15 minutes **MAKES:** 6 to 8 servings

Nonstick cooking spray

1 large onion, chopped (1 cup)

1 medium green, red, or yellow sweet pepper, seeded and chopped

2 cloves garlic, minced

1 14½-ounce can diced tomatoes, undrained

1 8-ounce can tomato sauce

½ cup chopped thinly sliced cooked turkey pepperoni

1 4-ounce can sliced mushrooms, drained (optional)

1 tablespoon snipped fresh oregano or basil or 1 teaspoon dried oregano or basil, crushed

⅛ to ¼ teaspoon crushed red pepper (optional)

8 to 10 ounces dried pasta

⅓ cup shredded Parmesan cheese

Fresh oregano (optional)

ONE Coat a large saucepan with cooking spray. Heat over medium heat. Add onion, sweet pepper, and garlic; cook until vegetables are tender, stirring occasionally. Stir in undrained tomatoes; tomato sauce; pepperoni; mushrooms, if desired; dried oregano, if using; and (if desired) crushed red pepper. Bring to boiling; reduce heat. Simmer, uncovered, about 10 minutes or until desired consistency, stirring occasionally.

TWO Meanwhile, cook pasta according to package directions; drain. Just before serving, stir in fresh oregano, if using. Serve over hot cooked pasta. Sprinkle with cheese. If desired, garnish with fresh oregano.

Nutrition Facts per serving: 234 cal., 4 g total fat (1 g sat. fat), 20 mg chol., 572 mg sodium, 38 g carbo. (5 g sugar), 2 g fiber, 11 g pro.
Exchanges: 1 Vegetable, 2 Starch, ½ Lean Meat, ½ Fat

get active

On a rainy or snowy day, head to the bowling alley. Most alleys have automatic scoring so you can just relax and bowl.

TACO PIZZA

photo, p. 106-107

PREP: 30 minutes **BAKE:** 16 minutes **OVEN:** 425°F **MAKES:** 8 servings

Nonstick cooking spray

1 1-pound loaf frozen whole wheat bread dough, thawed

1 cup shredded cheddar cheese (4 ounces)

12 ounces lean ground beef

1 medium onion, chopped (1/2 cup)

2/3 cup Easy Fresh Salsa (see recipe, page 121) or bottled salsa

2 medium tomatoes, chopped (1 1/2 cups)

1/2 to 1 cup shredded lettuce and/or spinach

1 cup packaged baked tortilla chips, coarsely crushed

Light dairy sour cream (optional)

Easy Fresh Salsa (see recipe, page 121) or bottled salsa (optional)

ONE Lightly coat a 12- to 13-inch pizza pan with nonstick cooking spray. Pat dough evenly into prepared pan, extending edges over pan slightly. (If dough is hard to pat out, let rest for 10 minutes.) Sprinkle half of the cheese in a thin strip around the edge of the dough. Moisten edge of dough. Fold edge over cheese and seal tightly to enclose the cheese. Prick crust all over with a fork. Bake in a 425° oven for 10 minutes.

TWO Meanwhile, in a large skillet cook beef and onion until beef is brown and onion is tender. Drain off fat. Stir in 2/3 cup Easy Fresh Salsa. Spoon beef mixture over crust. Bake for 5 minutes more. Sprinkle with tomatoes and remaining cheese. Bake for 1 to 2 minutes more or until cheese melts.

THREE To serve, cut pizza into 8 servings. Top with lettuce and/or spinach and tortilla chips. If desired, serve with sour cream and additional Easy Fresh Salsa.

Nutrition Facts per serving: 301 cal., 11 g total fat (5 g sat. fat), 42 mg chol., 437 mg sodium, 32 g carbo. (2 g sugar), 3 g fiber, 19 g pro.
Exchanges: 1/2 Vegetable, 2 Starch, 2 Lean Meat, 1/2 Fat

GRILLED VEGETABLE PIZZAS

PREP: 25 minutes **GRILL:** 11 minutes **MAKES:** 4 servings

- 1 **small yellow summer squash, quartered lengthwise**
- 1 **small red sweet pepper, quartered lengthwise**
- 1 **medium zucchini, quartered lengthwise**

  Nonstick cooking spray
- 1 **teaspoon black pepper**
- ½ **teaspoon salt**
- 1 **large tomato, seeded and chopped**
- ¼ **cup light mayonnaise or salad dressing**
- 2 **tablespoons purchased basil pesto**
- 1 **tablespoon snipped fresh basil**
- 1 **tablespoon snipped fresh oregano**
- 4 **6- to 7-inch flour tortillas**
- ¾ **cup shredded mozzarella or provolone cheese (3 ounces)**

ONE Lightly coat squash, sweet pepper, and zucchini with nonstick spray; sprinkle with black pepper and salt. For a charcoal grill, place vegetables on the rack of a grill with a cover directly over medium coals. Grill, uncovered, until crisp-tender, turning once halfway through grilling. Allow 5 to 6 minutes for squash and zucchini and 8 to 10 minutes for sweet pepper. Remove vegetables from grill.

TWO Chop grilled vegetables. In a medium bowl combine chopped vegetables, tomato, mayonnaise, pesto, basil, and oregano. Place tortillas on grill rack directly over heat. Cover and grill for 1 to 2 minutes or until lightly toasted on one side. Turn tortillas over and spread the vegetable mixture over the toasted sides of tortillas. Sprinkle with shredded cheese.

THREE Cover and grill for 2 to 3 minutes more or until tortillas are lightly toasted, vegetables are heated, and cheese begins to melt. Carefully remove from grill. (For a gas grill, preheat grill. Reduce heat to medium. Place vegetables and then tortillas over heat. Cover and grill as above.)

Nutrition Facts per serving: 277 cal., 17 g total fat (3 g sat. fat), 20 mg chol., 799 mg sodium, 23 g carbo. (5 g sugar), 2 g fiber, 11 g pro.
Exchanges: 1 Vegetable, 1 Starch, 1 Medium-Fat Meat, 2 Fat

CHICKEN PIZZA WITH A KICK

PREP: 25 minutes **BAKE:** 13 minutes **OVEN:** 400°F **MAKES:** 6 servings

12 ounces skinless, boneless chicken breast halves, cut into thin strips

2 teaspoons cooking oil

1 medium red sweet pepper, cut into thin strips

½ of a medium red onion, thinly sliced

Nonstick cooking spray

1 10-ounce package refrigerated pizza dough

½ cup bottled mild picante sauce or taco sauce

½ cup shredded sharp cheddar cheese (2 ounces)

ONE In a large nonstick skillet cook chicken strips in hot oil over medium-high heat about 5 minutes or until no longer pink. Remove from skillet. Add sweet pepper and onion to skillet; cook about 5 minutes or until tender. Remove from skillet; set aside.

TWO Coat a 15X10X1-inch baking pan with nonstick cooking spray. Unroll pizza dough into pan; press with fingers to form a 12X8-inch rectangle. Pinch edges of dough to form crust.

THREE Spread crust with picante sauce. Top with chicken and vegetables; sprinkle with cheddar cheese. Bake in a 400° oven for 13 to 18 minutes or until crust is brown and cheese melts.

Nutrition Facts per serving: 305 cal., 9 g total fat (3 g sat. fat), 43 mg chol., 527 mg sodium, 34 g carbo. (1 g sugar), 2 g fiber, 21 g pro.
Exchanges: ½ Vegetable, 2 Starch, 2 Lean Meat, ½ Fat

cut the sugar

A packet of taco seasoning usually contains added sugar that isn't needed. Try this sugar-free version instead.

CHICKEN TACOS

START TO FINISH: 27 minutes **MAKES:** 6 servings

Nonstick cooking spray

1 **cup chopped onion**

1 **clove garlic, minced**

2 **cups chopped cooked chicken**

1 **8-ounce can tomato sauce**

1 **4-ounce can diced green chile peppers, drained**

½ **teaspoon chili powder (optional)**

¼ **teaspoon ground cumin (optional)**

12 **taco shells or twelve 6- to 8-inch corn or flour tortillas, warmed**

2 **cups shredded lettuce**

1 **medium tomato, seeded and chopped**

½ **cup finely shredded reduced-fat cheddar cheese and/or Monterey Jack cheese (2 ounces)**

ONE Coat a large skillet with nonstick cooking spray. Heat over medium heat. Add onion and garlic; cook about 5 minutes or until onion is tender, stirring occasionally.

TWO Stir in chicken, tomato sauce, chile peppers, and (if desired) chili powder and ground cumin. Cook and stir until heated through.

THREE Divide chicken mixture among taco shells. Top with lettuce, tomato, and cheese.

TO WARM TORTILLAS: Wrap tortillas tightly in foil. Heat in a 350°F oven about 10 minutes or until heated through.

Nutrition Facts per serving: 27 cal., 12 g total fat (3 g sat. fat), 48 mg chol., 434 mg sodium, 23 g carbo. (3 g sugar), 3 g fiber, 19 g pro.
Exchanges: ½ Vegetable, 1½ Starch, 2 Lean Meat, 1 Fat

SOFT-SHELL BEEF BURRITOS

START TO FINISH: 35 minutes **OVEN:** 350°F **MAKES:** 6 servings

6 **8-inch plain flour tortillas**

12 **ounces lean ground beef**

½ **cup chopped onion (1 medium)**

2 **cloves garlic, minced**

½ **cup chopped green sweet pepper (1 small)**

½ **cup Easy Fresh Salsa (see recipe, page 121) or bottled salsa**

2 **teaspoons dried Mexican seasoning**

1½ **cups shredded lettuce**

1 **cup chopped tomatoes (2 medium)**

½ **cup shredded reduced-fat cheddar or Monterey Jack cheese (2 ounces)**

Shredded reduced-fat cheddar or Monterey Jack cheese (optional)

Easy Fresh Salsa (see recipe, page 121) or bottled salsa (optional)

ONE Wrap tortillas in foil; bake in a 350° oven about 10 minutes or until warmed.

TWO Meanwhile, in a large skillet cook ground beef, onion, and garlic over medium-high heat until beef is brown and onion is tender. Drain off fat. Stir in sweet pepper, ½ cup Easy Fresh Salsa, and Mexican seasoning. Bring to boiling; reduce heat. Simmer, covered, for 10 minutes.

THREE Top each tortilla with about ½ cup of the beef mixture and some of the lettuce and tomatoes. Sprinkle with some of the ½ cup cheese. Fold in sides; roll up. Cut in half to serve. If desired, sprinkle with additional cheese and pass additional Easy Fresh Salsa.

Nutrition Facts per serving: 230 cal., 10 g total fat (4 g sat. fat), 42 mg chol., 248 mg sodium, 20 g carbo. (3 g sugar), 2 g fiber, 16 g pro.
Exchanges: ½ Vegetable, 1 Starch, 2 Lean Meat, ½ Fat

SALSA, BEANS, AND MORE NACHOS

START TO FINISH: 33 minutes **OVEN:** 375°F **MAKES:** 6 appetizer servings

4 8-inch jalapeño, tomato, whole wheat, and/or plain flour tortillas

½ of a 16-ounce can fat-free refried beans (scant 1 cup)

¼ cup Easy Fresh Salsa (see recipe, page 121)

⅛ teaspoon ground cumin

½ cup shredded cheddar cheese

¾ cup shredded lettuce

½ cup Easy Fresh Salsa

Chopped avocado, light dairy sour cream, and/or snipped fresh cilantro (optional)

ONE Cut each tortilla into 8 wedges; spread wedges on 2 large cookie sheets. Bake in a 375° oven for 8 to 10 minutes or until dry and crisp. Cool on wire racks.

TWO Meanwhile, in a medium saucepan combine refried beans, ¼ cup Easy Fresh Salsa, and cumin. Cook and stir over medium-low heat until heated through.

THREE Spread cooled tortilla chips into 6 small baking dishes or a 3-quart au gratin or baking dish. Spoon bean mixture on top of tortillas. Sprinkle with cheese. Bake, uncovered, for 5 minutes or until cheese melts. Top with lettuce and ½ cup Easy Fresh Salsa. If desired, top with avocado, sour cream, and/or cilantro.

TIP: You may substitute 2 ounces of purchased baked tortilla chips for the tortillas. Prepare as directed above, starting with Step 2.

TIP: For a heartier dish, sprinkle 1 cup chopped cooked chicken on top of beans before adding cheese. Continue as directed.

Nutrition Facts per serving: 138 cal., 5 g total fat (2 g sat. fat), 10 mg chol., 297 mg sodium, 17 g carbo. (1 g sugar), 3 g fiber, 6 g pro.
Exchanges: 1 Starch, ½ Very Lean Meat, 1 Fat

CHEESE AND BEAN QUESADILLAS

START TO FINISH: 20 minutes **MAKES:** 4 servings

¼ **cup canned fat-free refried beans**

4 **6- to 8-inch flour tortillas**

¾ **cup shredded reduced-fat sharp cheddar cheese (3 ounces)**

Bottled salsa (optional)

ONE Spread 1 tablespoon of refried beans on half of a tortilla. Place bean-topped tortilla, bean side up, in a medium skillet or on a griddle. Sprinkle with one-fourth of the cheese.

TWO Cook over medium heat about 3 minutes or until cheese begins to melt. Fold tortilla in half. Turn and cook 1 to 2 minutes more or until golden brown. Repeat with remaining refried beans, tortillas, and cheese.

THREE To serve, cut each quesadilla into thirds. If desired, serve with salsa.

Nutrition Facts per serving: 148 cal., 5 g total fat (3 g sat. fat), 15 mg chol., 300 mg sodium, 14 g carbo. (0 g sugar), 1 g fiber, 8 g pro.
Exchanges: 1 Starch, ½ Medium-Fat Meat, ½ Fat

EASY FRESH SALSA

START TO FINISH: 20 minutes MAKES: 1²/₃ cups

2   medium tomatoes, seeded and chopped

¹/₄ cup finely chopped red onion

¹/₄ cup chopped yellow and/or green
     sweet pepper

2   to 3 teaspoons snipped fresh cilantro

1   clove garlic, minced

     Dash black pepper

     Few drops bottled hot pepper
     sauce (optional)

     Salt

ONE In a medium bowl combine tomatoes,
onion, sweet pepper, cilantro, garlic, black
pepper, and, if desired, hot pepper sauce.
Season to taste with salt. Serve immediately
or cover and chill for up to 3 days. Stir
before serving.

Nutrition Facts per ¹/₃-cup: 17 cal., 0 g total fat
(0 g sat. fat), 0 mg chol., 31 mg sodium, 4 g carbo.
(2 g sugar), 1 g fiber, 1 g pro.
Exchanges: Free

cut the sugar

Because it uses fresh
ingredients, salsa shouldn't
contain sugar. Although
it's a small amount,
store-bought salsas have
unneeded sugar, while this
Easy Fresh Salsa doesn't.

get active

Give badminton a try when the weather is nice. Even little kids can play, making it perfect for families.

ITALIAN VEGGIE BURGER BITES

START TO FINISH: 15 minutes **MAKES:** 1 serving

1 **refrigerated or frozen meatless burger patty**

1 **tablespoon tomato paste**

3 **to 4 teaspoons water**

½ **teaspoon snipped fresh basil**

2 **slices firm-textured whole wheat or oatmeal bread, toasted, if desired**

1 **slice mozzarella cheese (1 ounce)**

4 **small fresh basil leaves**

ONE Cook burger patty according to package directions. Meanwhile, for sauce, in a small bowl combine tomato paste, water, and snipped basil.

TWO To serve, place burger patty on 1 slice of bread. Top with sauce, cheese, and basil leaves. Top with another slice of bread. Cut into quarters.

Nutrition Facts per serving: 332 cal., 12 g total fat (2 g sat. fat), 25 mg chol., 819 mg sodium, 33 g carbo. (11 g sugar), 8 g fiber, 26 g pro.
Exchanges: 2 Starch, 2 Lean Meat

TOMATO-MAYO VEGGIE BURGER BITES: Prepare as above except omit tomato paste, water, basil, and cheese. In a small bowl combine 2 teaspoons low-carb catsup, 1 tablespoon light mayonnaise, and a dash garlic powder. Top burger with the catsup mixture and a lettuce leaf. Serve as above.

Nutrition Facts per serving: 289 cal., 11 g fat (2 g sat fat), 8 mg chol., 805 mg sodium, 33 g carbo. (12 g sugar), 7 g fiber, 19 g pro.
Exchanges: 2 Starch, 2 Lean Meat, ½ Fat

BARBECUE VEGGIE BURGER BITES: Prepare as above except omit tomato paste, water, basil, and cheese. Top burger with a rounded tablespoon Barbecue Sauce (see recipe, page 90) and a lettuce leaf. Serve as above.

Nutrition Facts per serving: 253 cal., 6 g fat (2 g sat fat), 3 mg chol., 736 mg sodium, 32 g carbo. (11 g sugar), 8 g fiber, 20 g pro.
Exchanges: 2 Starch, 2 Lean Meat

VERY VEGGIE BURGER BITES: Prepare as above except omit tomato paste, water, basil, and cheese. Top burger with a rounded tablespoon Very Veggie Dip (see recipe, page 21) and a lettuce leaf. Serve as above.

Nutrition Facts per serving: 255 cal., 7 g fat (2 g sat fat), 8 mg chol., 664 mg sodium, 30 g carbo. (11 g sugar), 8 g fiber, 20 g pro.
Exchanges: 2 Starch, 2 Lean Meat

OVEN-ROASTED CHEESE FRIES

PREP: 10 minutes **BAKE:** 22 minutes **OVEN:** 450°F **MAKES:** 6 servings

 4 **teaspoons olive oil**

 4 **medium baking potatoes
    (1½ pounds total), scrubbed**

 ½ **teaspoon salt**

 ⅛ **to ¼ teaspoon freshly ground
    black pepper**

 ¼ **cup grated Parmesan cheese (1 ounce)**

ONE Line a 15X10X1-inch baking pan with heavy-duty foil; brush with 2 teaspoons of the oil. Set aside.

TWO Cut potatoes lengthwise into ½-inch-thick wedges. Transfer to a large bowl. Add remaining 2 teaspoons oil; toss to coat. Sprinkle potato wedges with salt and pepper, tossing to coat. Arrange potato wedges in a single layer in prepared baking pan.

THREE Bake in a 450° oven for 12 minutes. Carefully turn potato wedges; sprinkle with cheese. Bake for 10 to 12 minutes more or until potatoes are tender and golden. Serve immediately.

Nutrition Facts per serving: 105 cal., 4 g total fat (1 g sat. fat), 3 mg chol., 262 mg sodium, 14 g carbo. (1 g sugar), 1 g fiber, 3 g pro.
Exchanges: 1 Starch, ½ Fat

cut the sugar

Just 1 tablespoon of catsup has 4 grams of sugar. Multiply that by several servings (which is easy when dipping fries), and that sugar adds up fast.

CHICKEN NUGGETS

PREP: 20 minutes **BAKE:** 7 minutes **OVEN:** 450°F **MAKES:** 4 servings

- ²/₃ **cup crushed cornflakes**
- 1 **teaspoon paprika**
- ½ **teaspoon garlic powder**
- ½ **teaspoon dried oregano, crushed**
- ⅛ **teaspoon cayenne pepper (optional)**
- 1 **slightly beaten egg white**
- 1 **pound skinless, boneless chicken breast halves, cut into 1-inch pieces**

ONE In a plastic bag combine crushed cornflakes, paprika, garlic powder, oregano, and (if desired) cayenne pepper. Place egg white in a small bowl.

TWO Dip chicken pieces into egg white, allowing excess to drain off. Add pieces, a few at a time, to cornflake mixture; shake to coat well.

THREE Place chicken pieces in a single layer in a shallow baking pan. Bake in a 450° oven for 7 to 9 minutes or until chicken is no longer pink.

Nutrition Facts per serving: 191 cal., 2 g total fat (0 g sat. fat), 66 mg chol., 228 mg sodium, 13 g carbo. (1 g sugar), 0 g fiber, 29 g pro.
Exchanges: 1 Starch, 3½ Very Lean Meat

PEPPERS AND SNOW PEAS NOODLE BOWL

START TO FINISH: 25 minutes **MAKES:** 4 servings

- 2 **cups dried Chinese egg noodles or fine egg noodles (4 ounces)**
- ¼ **teaspoon ground ginger**
- ⅓ **cup bottled stir-fry sauce**
- 1 **cup snow pea pods or fresh sugar snap peas, tips and stems removed, and cut up**
- 1 **medium red sweet pepper, cut into bite-size strips**
- 2 **teaspoons peanut oil or cooking oil**
- 5 **ounces cooked chicken breast, cut into strips (about 1 cup)**
- 2 **tablespoons coarsely chopped cashews or peanuts or sliced almonds, toasted**

ONE Cook noodles according to package directions. Drain; set aside. In a small bowl stir ginger into the bottled stir-fry sauce; set aside.

TWO In a large skillet cook and stir peas and sweet pepper in hot oil over medium-high heat for 3 to 5 minutes or until crisp-tender. Add cooked noodles, chicken, stir-fry sauce, and cashews; heat through.

Nutrition Facts per serving: 235 cal., 7 g total fat (1 g sat. fat), 49 mg chol., 540 mg sodium, 24 g carbo. (2 g sugar), 3 g fiber, 18 g pro.
Exchanges: ½ Vegetable, 1 Starch, ½ Other Carbo., 1½ Very Lean Meat, 1 Fat

cut the sugar

Teriyaki or soy sauces, common in Asian foods, are notoriously high in sugar—almost 3 grams per serving.

SWEET-AND-SOUR CHICKEN

START TO FINISH: 30 minutes **MAKES:** 6 servings

¾ cup reduced-sodium chicken broth

3 tablespoons red wine vinegar

2 tablespoons reduced-sodium soy sauce

4 teaspoons sugar

1 tablespoon cornstarch

1 clove garlic, minced

2 medium carrots, thinly sliced

1 medium red sweet pepper, cut into bite-size strips (1 cup)

4 teaspoons cooking oil

1 cup fresh pea pods, tips and stems removed

12 ounces skinless, boneless chicken breast halves, cut into 1-inch pieces

1 8-ounce can pineapple chunks (juice pack), drained

3 cups hot cooked rice

ONE For sauce, in a small bowl stir together chicken broth, vinegar, soy sauce, sugar, cornstarch, and garlic; set aside.

TWO In a large nonstick skillet cook and stir carrots and sweet pepper in 3 teaspoons of the hot oil over medium-high heat for 3 minutes. Add pea pods. Cook and stir about 1 minute more or until vegetables are crisp-tender. Remove from skillet; set aside.

THREE Add remaining 1 teaspoon oil to skillet. Add chicken to skillet. Cook and stir for 3 to 4 minutes or until chicken is no longer pink. Push chicken from center of skillet. Stir sauce; add to center of skillet. Cook and stir until thickened and bubbly. Add vegetable mixture and pineapple chunks; heat through. Serve with hot cooked rice.

Nutrition Facts per serving: 259 cal., 4 g total fat (1 g sat. fat), 33 mg chol., 311 mg sodium, 37 g carbo. (11 g sugar), 2 g fiber, 17 g pro.
Exchanges: ½ Vegetable, 1½ Starch, 1 Other Carbo., 2 Very Lean Meat

GINGER BEEF STIR-FRY

START TO FINISH: 30 minutes **MAKES:** 4 servings

8 ounces beef top round steak

½ cup reduced-sodium beef broth

3 tablespoons reduced-sodium soy sauce

2½ teaspoons cornstarch

1 teaspoon grated fresh ginger

Nonstick cooking spray

3 cups small broccoli florets or 1 pound fresh asparagus spears, trimmed and cut into 2-inch pieces

1½ cups sliced fresh mushrooms or thinly sliced carrots

4 green onions, bias-sliced into 2-inch lengths (½ cup)

1 tablespoon cooking oil

2 cups hot cooked rice

ONE If desired, partially freeze beef for easier slicing. Trim fat from beef. Thinly slice beef across the grain into bite-size strips. Set aside. For the sauce, in a small bowl stir together beef broth, soy sauce, cornstarch, and ginger; set aside.

TWO Lightly coat an unheated wok or large skillet with nonstick cooking spray. Heat over medium-high heat. Add broccoli, mushrooms, and green onions. Stir-fry for 3 to 4 minutes or until vegetables are crisp-tender. Remove from wok or skillet.

THREE Carefully add oil to wok or skillet. Add beef; stir-fry for 2 to 3 minutes or until brown. Push beef from center of the wok or skillet. Stir sauce; add to center of wok or skillet. Cook and stir until thickened and bubbly.

FOUR Return vegetables to wok or skillet. Stir all ingredients together to coat with sauce; heat through. Serve immediately over hot cooked rice.

Nutrition Facts per serving: 31 cal., 7 g total fat (1 g sat. fat), 32 mg chol., 538 mg sodium, 31 g carbo. (2 g sugar), 3 g fiber, 19 g pro.
Exchanges: 1½ Vegetable, 1½ Starch, 1½ Lean Meat, ½ Fat

ASIAN SPRING ROLLS

START TO FINISH: 30 minutes **MAKES:** 4 servings (8 rolls)

8 8-inch round spring roll wrappers

8 ounces fresh or frozen cooked, peeled, and deveined shrimp, coarsely chopped (1⅓ cups)

1 small head Bibb lettuce, cored and shredded (2 cups)

1 cup shredded carrots (2 medium)

¼ cup sliced green onions (2)

2 tablespoons snipped fresh cilantro

1 recipe Peanut Sauce (see recipe, page 92)

1 tablespoon seasoned rice vinegar

   Hot water

ONE Place some warm water in a shallow dish. Dip each spring roll wrapper in warm water; place between damp paper towels for 10 minutes.

TWO Meanwhile, for filling, in a large bowl combine shrimp, lettuce, carrots, green onions, and cilantro. Add 2 tablespoons of the Peanut Sauce and the vinegar. Toss to coat.

THREE For the dipping sauce, in a small bowl whisk together remaining Peanut Sauce and enough hot water to make dipping consistency; set aside.

FOUR Place about ½ cup of the filling about ½ inch from the bottom edge of one of the moistened spring roll wrappers. Fold the bottom edge of the wrapper over the filling. Fold in sides. Roll up. Repeat with remaining filling and spring roll wrappers. Cut rolls in half; serve with dipping sauce.

Nutrition Facts per serving: 234 cal., 7 g total fat (1 g sat. fat), 111 mg chol., 402 mg sodium, 26 g carbo. (3 g sugar), 3 g fiber, 17 g pro.
Exchanges: 1 Vegetable, 1½ Starch, 1½ Very Lean Meat, 1 Fat

sweet so

Sweets with less sugar don't have to be sweet nothings. When you start with fresh fruits, nuts, milk, and grains, you end up with desserts high in nutrients that are so full of flavor your kids won't miss the sugar.

methings

WATERMELON FREEZE

PREP: 30 minutes **FREEZE:** 5 hours **STAND:** 30 minutes **MAKES:** 10 servings

¾ **cup water**

⅓ **cup sugar**

3 **cups seeded watermelon cubes**

2 **cups halved strawberries**

Fresh mint sprigs (optional)

Fresh strawberries (optional)

ONE In a small saucepan combine water and sugar; bring to boiling, stirring to dissolve sugar. Boil gently, uncovered, for 2 minutes. Remove from heat and cool slightly.

TWO Meanwhile, place watermelon and 2 cups strawberries in a blender container or food processor bowl; cover and blend or process until nearly smooth. Add warm sugar mixture and blend or process until smooth. Transfer mixture to a 3-quart rectangular baking dish or 3-quart freezer container. Cover and freeze about 3 hours or until almost firm (mixture may be slushy in center).

THREE Remove mixture from freezer. Using a fork, break up the frozen fruit mixture until almost smooth but not melted. Cover and freeze for 2 hours or overnight or until completely frozen.

FOUR To serve, let stand at room temperature for 30 minutes. Scoop or use a metal spoon to scrape mixture and spoon into dessert dishes to serve. If desired, top with mint sprigs and a few strawberries.

Nutrition Facts per serving: 47 cal., 0 g total fat (0 g sat. fat), 0 mg chol., 1 mg sodium, 12 g carbo. (11 g sugar), 1 g fiber, 0 g pro.
Exchanges: ½ Fruit, ½ Other Carbo.

TROPICAL FREEZE: Prepare as above except substitute 3 cups peeled orange sections (about 6 oranges) for the watermelon and substitute 2 cups fresh pineapple cubes for the strawberries. If desired, garnish with orange slices instead of the strawberries. Makes 10 servings.

Nutrition Facts per serving: 68 cal., 0 g total fat, (0 mg sat. fat) 0 mg chol., 2 mg sodium, 17 g carbo. (15 g sugar), 2 g fiber, 1 g pro.
Exchanges: ½ Fruit, ½ Other Carbo.

BLUEBERRY-MANGO FREEZE: Prepare as above except substitute 3 cups blueberries for the watermelon and 2 cups cubed, peeled mango or sliced, peeled kiwifruit for the strawberries. If desired, garnish with blueberries or mango or kiwifruit slices. Makes 10 servings.

Nutrition Facts per serving: 67 cal., 0 g fat (0 g sat. fat), 0 mg chol., 1 mg sodium, 17 g carbo. (14 g sugar), 3 g fiber, 0 g pro.
Exchanges: ½ Fruit, ½ Other Carbo.

SUPER COOL BERRY-BANANA TREAT

PREP: 15 minutes **MAKES:** 4 to 6 servings

- **2 cups fresh blueberries, frozen**
- **1 medium ripe banana, peeled, sliced, and frozen**
- **²/₃ cup fresh-squeezed orange juice**
- **Fresh blueberries (optional)**

ONE In a food processor bowl place 1 cup of the blueberries, half of the banana slices, and half of the orange juice. Cover and process until almost smooth. Transfer to a medium bowl. Repeat with remaining blueberries, banana slices, and orange juice. Serve immediately or transfer to a 1½-quart freezer container; cover and freeze for 1 hour. Stir before serving. If desired, serve with additional blueberries.

NOTE: To freeze blueberries and banana slices, place them in a single layer in a shallow baking pan. Freeze for 2 hours. When frozen, transfer fruit to a freezer container or plastic freezer bag and seal. Store in freezer for up to 12 months.

Nutrition Facts per serving: 80 cal., 0 g total fat (0 g sat. fat), 0 mg chol., 1 mg sodium, 19 g carbo. (9 g sugar), 4 g fiber, 1 g pro.
Exchanges: 1½ Fruit

get active

When watching television, get up and walk in place or do jumping jacks during the commercials.

TOP-YOUR-OWN ANGEL CAKE

PREP: 15 minutes **BAKE:** 20 minutes **OVEN:** 300°F **MAKES:** 6 servings

2 cups bite-size angel food cake cubes

2 cups no-sugar-added vanilla ice cream

2 cups fresh fruit, such as blueberries, raspberries, sliced strawberries, sliced kiwifruit, and/or cut-up peaches

ONE Place angel cake cubes in a single layer in a shallow baking pan. Bake in a 300° oven for 20 to 25 minutes or until golden brown, stirring occasionally. Remove from oven. Cool completely.

TWO In 6 serving dishes or parfait glasses layer angel cake cubes, ice cream, and fruit. Serve immediately.

Nutrition Facts per serving: 108 cal., 2 g total fat (1 g sat. fat), 7 mg chol., 105 mg sodium, 19 g carbo. (6 g sugar), 2 g fiber, 3 g pro. **Exchanges:** ½ Fruit, 1 Other Carbo.

STRAWBERRY-PRETZEL PARFAITS

PREP: 20 minutes **CHILL:** up to 4 hours **MAKES:** 4 servings

1 **8-ounce tub light cream cheese, softened**

1 **tablespoon fat-free milk**

1 **teaspoon vanilla**

1 **cup coarsely crushed pretzels**

1½ **cups sliced fresh strawberries**

ONE In a small bowl stir together cream cheese, milk, and vanilla until smooth. In four 8-ounce parfait glasses or drinking glasses, layer half the pretzels, half the cream cheese mixture, and half the strawberries. Repeat layers. Serve immediately or cover and chill for up to 4 hours before serving.

Nutrition Facts per serving: 188 cal., 9 g total fat (5 g sat. fat), 27 mg chol., 507 mg sodium, 20 g carbo. (11 g sugar), 2 g fiber, 8 g pro.
Exchanges: ½ Fruit, 1 Starch, 2 Fat

get active

Get up early and walk to school as a family. Both parents and kids will get a healthy start to the day.

CUSTARD PIE TOWERS

PREP: 25 minutes   **CHILL:** 2 hours   **MAKES:** 6 servings

4 **slightly beaten egg yolks**

1 **cup fat-free milk**

2 **tablespoons sugar**

1 **teaspoon vanilla**

½ **cup graham cracker crumbs**

¼ **cup finely chopped almonds, toasted**

⅛ **teaspoon ground cinnamon**

1½ **cups raspberries and/or sliced strawberries**

1½ **cups blueberries**

ONE For custard, in a small heavy saucepan stir together egg yolks, milk, and sugar. Cook and stir over medium heat until mixture is thickened and coats the back of a metal spoon (do not boil).

TWO Remove pan from heat. Quickly cool mixture by placing saucepan in a large bowl of ice water for 1 to 2 minutes, stirring constantly. Stir in vanilla. Pour mixture into a small bowl. Cover surface with plastic wrap to prevent a skin from forming. Chill for at least 2 hours or up to 24 hours before serving. Do not stir. (Custard will be thickened but will not be set.)

THREE In a small bowl combine graham cracker crumbs, almonds, and ground cinnamon.

FOUR Divide half of the graham cracker mixture among 6 tall 8-ounce glasses, small parfait glasses, or small dessert dishes. Layer with half of the raspberries and/or strawberries and half of the chilled custard. Top with half of the blueberries. Repeat layers. Serve immediately.

Nutrition Facts per serving: 157 cal., 6 g total fat (1 g sat. fat), 137 mg chol., 62 mg sodium, 19 g carbo. (11 g sugar), 5 g fiber, 5 g pro.
Exchanges: ½ Fruit, 1 Other Carbo., ½ Medium-Fat Meat, ½ Fat

PEACHY BERRY COBBLER

PREP: 35 minutes **BAKE:** 15 minutes **OVEN:** 400°F **MAKES:** 8 servings

1 **cup all-purpose flour**

1½ **teaspoons baking powder**

¼ **teaspoon ground ginger or ground cinnamon**

⅛ **teaspoon salt**

2 **tablespoons butter or margarine**

¼ **cup sugar**

4 **teaspoons cornstarch**

⅓ **cup water**

3 **cups fresh or frozen unsweetened peach slices**

2 **cups fresh or frozen unsweetened raspberries**

⅓ **cup plain fat-free yogurt**

1 **slightly beaten egg**

Ground ginger or ground cinnamon (optional)

ONE For topping, in a bowl stir together flour, baking powder, ¼ teaspoon ginger, and salt. Using a pastry blender, cut in butter until mixture resembles coarse crumbs. Set aside.

TWO For filling, in a large saucepan stir together sugar and cornstarch. Stir in water. Add peach slices and raspberries. Cook and stir until thickened and bubbly. Keep filling hot while finishing topping.

THREE To finish topping, stir together yogurt and egg. Add yogurt mixture to flour mixture, stirring just until moistened.

FOUR Divide filling among eight 6-ounce custard cups or four 10- to 12-ounce casseroles. Drop topping from a spoon onto hot filling. Drop 1 mound into each custard cup or 2 mounds into each casserole. Place custard cups or casseroles on a baking sheet.

FIVE Bake in a 400° oven for 15 to 20 minutes or until a wooden toothpick inserted into topping comes out clean. Cool slightly. If desired, sprinkle with additional ginger. Serve warm.

TIP: To make a large cobbler, transfer hot filling to a 2-quart square baking dish. Drop topping from a spoon into 8 mounds on top of hot filling. Bake in a 400°F oven about 20 minutes or until a wooden toothpick inserted into topping comes out clean.

Nutrition Facts per serving: 160 cal., 4 g total fat (2 g sat. fat), 35 mg chol., 120 mg sodium, 28 g carbo. (9 g sugar), 4 g fiber, 4 g pro.
Exchanges: ½ Fruit, 1 Starch, ½ Other Carbo., ½ Fat

cut the sugar

A store-bought peach cobbler mix has 16 grams of sugar per serving, while this Peachy Berry Cobbler recipe has about half that much per serving.

BURSTS OF COLOR FRUIT SALAD

PREP: 30 minutes **MAKES:** 6 servings

2 **cups sliced fresh peaches (peeled, if desired), nectarines, plums, and/or apricots**

2 **cups assorted fresh berries, such as halved strawberries, blackberries, blueberries, and/or raspberries**

2 **tablespoons orange juice**

1 **to 2 tablespoons sugar (optional)**

1 **cantaloupe, halved, seeded, and cut into 6 wedges**

ONE In a large bowl gently toss together peaches, nectarines, plums, and/or apricots, berries, orange juice, and (if desired) sugar. To serve, spoon mixture on top of cantaloupe wedges.

Nutrition Facts per serving: 73 cal., 0 g total fat (0 g sat. fat), 0 mg chol., 15 mg sodium, 18 g carbo. (10 g sugar), 3 g fiber, 1 g pro.
Exchanges: 1 Fruit

cut the sugar

Fruit taste sweeter when it's cooked, so these Fantastic Fruit Kabobs have a naturally sweet flavor without adding sugar.

FANTASTIC FRUIT KABOBS

PREP: 20 minutes **GRILL:** 6 minutes **MAKES:** 6 servings

¼ **teaspoon ground cinnamon**

¼ **teaspoon ground ginger**

⅛ **teaspoon ground cardamom or ground nutmeg**

2 **medium plums, halved and pitted**

1 **large firm ripe peach or nectarine, halved and pitted**

½ **of a small fresh pineapple (1 pound)**

1 **medium firm ripe banana, peeled and cut into 1-inch slices**

1 **cup Creamy Fruit Dip (see recipe, page 48)**

ONE In a small bowl combine cinnamon, ginger, and cardamom; set aside. For kabobs, cut each plum half into 2 wedges. Cut each peach half into 3 or 4 wedges. If desired, peel pineapple. Cut pineapple into 1-inch slices; cut each slice into 8 wedges. Alternately thread pieces of fruit on 6 long metal or wooden skewers. Sprinkle cinnamon mixture evenly over kabobs.

TWO For a charcoal grill, grill kabobs on the rack of an uncovered grill directly over medium coals for 6 to 8 minutes or until heated through, turning once. (For a gas grill, preheat grill. Reduce heat to medium. Place kabobs on grill rack over heat. Cover and grill as above.)

THREE Serve warm fruit with Creamy Fruit Dip.

TO BROIL KABOBS: Place kabobs on the unheated rack of a broiler pan. Broil 5 to 6 inches from the heat for 6 to 8 minutes or until heated through, turning once.

TIP: If using wooden skewers, soak them in water for at least 1 hour before grilling or broiling.

Nutrition Facts per serving: 142 cal., 5 g total fat (3 g sat. fat), 18 mg chol., 77 mg sodium, 21 g carbo. (15 g sugar), 2 g fiber, 4 g pro.
Exchanges: 1 Fruit, ½ Other Carbo., 1 Fat

APPLES AND PEANUT BUTTER CRISP

PREP: 20 minutes **BAKE:** 30 minutes **OVEN:** 375°F **MAKES:** 8 servings

6 **medium red and/or green cooking apples, cored, peeled, if desired, and thinly sliced**

2 **tablespoons all-purpose flour**

1 **tablespoon packed brown sugar**

²/₃ **cup quick-cooking rolled oats**

2 **tablespoons all-purpose flour**

2 **tablespoons packed brown sugar**

¼ **cup peanut butter**

2 **tablespoons chopped peanuts**

ONE Place apple slices in a 2-quart square baking dish; set aside. In a small bowl stir together 2 tablespoons flour and 1 tablespoon brown sugar until well combined. Sprinkle over apple slices in dish; toss to coat.

TWO Bake, covered, in a 375° oven for 15 minutes. Meanwhile, in a medium bowl combine rolled oats, 2 tablespoons flour, and 2 tablespoons brown sugar. Using a fork, stir in peanut butter until mixture resembles coarse crumbs. Stir in peanuts.

THREE Uncover apple mixture; sprinkle with oat mixture. Bake, uncovered, for 15 to 20 minutes more or until apples are tender and topping is golden. Serve warm.

Nutrition Facts per serving: 174 cal., 6 g total fat (1 g sat. fat), 0 mg chol., 51 mg sodium, 28 g carbo. (17 g sugar), 4 g fiber, 4 g pro.
Exchanges: 1 Fruit, ½ Starch, ½ Other Carbo., ½ High-Fat Meat

cut the sugar

Apple crisp from a box mix has 23 grams of sugar. Try this Apples and Peanut Butter Crisp instead.

OATMEAL-BANANA BREAD PUDDING

PREP: 20 minutes **BAKE:** 35 minutes **OVEN:** 350°F **MAKES:** 9 servings

- **2 cups fat-free milk**
- **2 slightly beaten eggs**
- **3 tablespoons packed brown sugar**
- **1 teaspoon vanilla**
- **½ teaspoon pumpkin pie spice or ground cinnamon**
- **5 cups dry oatmeal bread cubes**
- **2 medium bananas, halved lengthwise and sliced**
- **½ cup chopped walnuts or pecans, toasted (optional)**

ONE In a medium bowl whisk together milk, eggs, brown sugar, vanilla, and pumpkin pie spice; set aside. In a 2-quart square baking dish toss together bread cubes, banana slices, and, if desired, walnuts. Pour egg mixture evenly over bread mixture. Toss until bread is moistened.

TWO Bake in a 350° oven for 35 to 40 minutes or until a knife inserted near the center comes out clean. Cool slightly before serving.

TO DRY BREAD CUBES: Spread 8½ cups bread cubes (11 slices) in a shallow baking pan. Bake in a 300°F oven for 10 to 15 minutes or until bread cubes are dry, stirring twice; cool.

Nutrition Facts per serving: 167 cal., 3 g total fat (1 g sat. fat), 48 mg chol., 239 mg sodium, 30 g carbo. (14 g sugar), 2 g fiber, 6 g pro.
Exchanges: ½ Fruit, 1 Starch, ½ Other Carbo., ½ Fat

cut the sugar

A regular bread pudding recipe can contain more than double the amount of sugar in this Oatmeal-Banana Bread Pudding.

PEANUT BUTTER-BANANA CREPES

START TO FINISH: 30 minutes **MAKES:** 9 servings

1 slightly beaten egg

¾ cup fat-free milk

½ cup all-purpose flour

1 teaspoon cooking oil

⅛ teaspoon salt

1 cup Peanut Butter Dip
(see recipe, page 48)

3 medium bananas, sliced

ONE In a medium bowl combine egg, milk, flour, oil, and salt; beat until combined. Heat a lightly greased 6-inch nonstick skillet over medium heat. Remove from heat. Spoon in 2 tablespoons batter; lift and tilt skillet to spread batter. Return to heat; brown on one side only. (Or cook on a crepe maker according to manufacturer's directions.) Invert skillet over paper towels; remove crepe. Repeat with remaining batter, greasing skillet occasionally.

TWO Spread Peanut Butter Dip down center of each crepe. Top with banana slices. Fold sides of crepes up over bananas.

Nutrition Facts per serving: 152 cal., 7 g total fat (3 g sat. fat), 35 mg chol., 125 mg sodium, 17 g carbo. (7 g sugar), 2 g fiber, 6 g pro.
Exchanges: ½ Fruit, ½ Other Carbo., 1 High-Fat Meat, 1 Fat

STRAWBERRIES AND CREME CREPES: Prepare crepes as above except substitute Creamy Fruit Dip (see recipe, page 48) for the Peanut Butter Dip and substitute 3 cups sliced strawberries for the bananas.

Nutrition Facts per serving: 104 cal., 5 g fat (2 g sat. fat), 36 mg chol., 67 mg sodium, 12 g carbo. (4 g sugar), 1 g fiber, 4 g pro.
Exchanges: ½ Fruit, ½ Other Carbo., 1 Fat.

PILED-HIGH SHORTCAKE

PREP: 25 minutes **BAKE:** 7 minutes **OVEN:** 425°F **MAKES:** 6 servings

- ¾ **cup all-purpose flour**
- 2 **teaspoons sugar**
- 1 **teaspoon baking powder**
- ⅛ **teaspoon baking soda**
  Dash salt
- 2 **tablespoons butter**
- ¼ **cup buttermilk**
- 1 **slightly beaten egg yolk**
  Nonstick cooking spray
- ½ **of an 8-ounce package reduced-fat cream cheese (Neufchâtel), softened**
- 1 **8-ounce carton plain low-fat yogurt**
- 3 **tablespoons low-sugar strawberry preserves**
- 1½ **cups fresh raspberries, blackberries, blueberries, cut up nectarines, and/or peeled and cut up kiwifruit**

ONE For shortcakes, in a medium bowl stir together flour, sugar, baking powder, baking soda, and salt. Using a pastry blender, cut in butter until mixture resembles coarse crumbs. Make a well in center of flour mixture. In a small bowl combine buttermilk and egg yolk. Add to flour mixture all at once, stirring just until moistened.

TWO Lightly coat a baking sheet with nonstick cooking spray; set aside. On a lightly floured surface, pat or roll dough to ½-inch thickness. Using a floured 1½- to 2-inch cookie cutter, cut dough into desired shapes, rerolling scraps as necessary. Place on prepared baking sheet. Bake in a 425° oven for 7 to 8 minutes or until golden. Cool on a wire rack.

THREE In a medium mixing bowl beat cream cheese with an electric mixer on medium speed for 30 seconds. Gradually beat in yogurt and preserves until smooth.

FOUR Divide shortcakes among 6 dessert plates; top with fresh fruit and yogurt mixture. Serve immediately.

Nutrition Facts per serving: 212 cal., 10 g total fat (6 g sat. fat), 62 mg chol., 232 mg sodium, 25 g carbo. (11 g sugar), 1 g fiber, 6 g pro.
Exchanges: 1½ Other Carbo., 2 Fat

APPLE-CINNAMON SQUARES photo, p. 133

PREP: 25 minutes **BAKE:** 10 minutes **OVEN:** 350°F **MAKES:** 12 servings

¼ **cup butter or margarine, softened**

⅓ **cup packed brown sugar**

¼ **teaspoon baking soda**

1 **egg**

1 **teaspoon vanilla**

½ **cup all-purpose flour**

⅔ **cup quick-cooking rolled oats**

Thin apple slices

¾ **cup Apple-Cinnamon Dip**
(see recipe, page 48)

½ **cup Honey-Orange Granola**
(see recipe, page 47)

ONE Line an 8X8X2-inch baking pan with foil, extending foil over sides of pan; set aside. In a large mixing bowl beat butter with an electric mixer on medium to high speed for 30 seconds. Beat in brown sugar and baking soda until combined. Beat in egg and vanilla. Beat in as much of the flour as you can with the mixer. Stir in any remaining flour and the oats.

TWO Lightly press dough into prepared pan. Bake in a 350° oven for 10 to 12 minutes or until top is set and edges are firm. Let cool in pan on a wire rack.

THREE Lift cookie square from pan using foil. Peel off foil. Cut cookie into 12 squares. Just before serving, top cookie squares with apple slices and a spoonful of the Apple-Cinnamon Dip. Sprinkle with Honey-Orange Granola.

Nutrition Facts per serving: 158 cal., 7 g total fat (4 g sat. fat), 36 mg chol., 101 mg sodium, 20 g carbo. (10 g sugar), 2 g fiber, 3 g pro.
Exchanges: 1½ Other Carbo., 1 Fat

CHOCOLATE-PEANUT BUTTER-SWIRL DESSERT

PREP: 20 minutes **CHILL:** 2 hours **MAKES:** 12 servings

- **1 cup graham cracker crumbs**
- **½ cup finely chopped peanuts**
- **3 tablespoons butter, melted**
- **¼ cup tub-style light cream cheese**
- **2 tablespoons creamy peanut butter**
- **2 tablespoons fat-free milk**
- **2 cups fat-free milk**
- **1 4-serving-size package sugar-free instant chocolate pudding mix**

ONE In a medium bowl combine graham cracker crumbs and chopped peanuts. Stir in butter until combined. Reserve 3 tablespoons of the mixture; set aside. Press remaining mixture into the bottom of 2-quart square baking dish. Cover and chill while preparing filling.

TWO In a small bowl stir together cream cheese and peanut butter until smooth. Gradually stir in 2 tablespoons milk until smooth. Set aside.

THREE In a large bowl whisk together 2 cups milk and pudding mix until combined. Continue whisking for 2 minutes. Spread over graham cracker crust in pan. Drop peanut butter mixture in small mounds on top of pudding. Using a thin metal spatula or table knife, gently swirl peanut butter mixture into pudding. Sprinkle with reserved crumb mixture.

FOUR Cover and chill about 2 hours or until set. To serve, spoon into dessert dishes.

Nutrition Facts per serving: 147 cal., 9 g total fat (3 g sat. fat), 11 mg chol., 247 mg sodium, 12 g carbo. (3 g sugar), 1 g fiber, 5 g pro.
Exchanges: 1 Other Carbo., 1½ Fat

CHOCOLATE-MINT CUPS

PREP: 20 minutes **CHILL:** 2 hours **MAKES:** 6 servings

1 4-serving-size package sugar-free instant chocolate pudding mix

2 cups fat-free milk

¼ of an 8-ounce container frozen light or regular whipped dessert topping, thawed

⅛ to ¼ teaspoon mint extract

Green or red food coloring (optional)

Whipped topping (optional)

Sprig fresh mint (optional)

ONE Prepare pudding mix according to package directions using the 2 cups fat-free milk. Set aside. In a small bowl combine dessert topping, mint extract, and (if desired) food coloring to make desired color.

TWO In 6 small dessert bowls layer half the pudding, followed by dessert topping and remaining pudding. Cover and chill for 2 hours or until set. If desired, top with whipped topping and mint.

Nutrition Facts per serving: 73 cal., 1 g total fat (1 g sat. fat), 2 mg chol., 256 mg sodium, 11 g carbo. (5 g sugar), 0 g fiber, 3 g pro.
Exchanges: 1 Other Carbo.

get active

Plant a family garden with everyone in charge of their own patch of fruits, vegetables, and flowers.

CHOCOLATE CHIP COOKIES

PREP: 20 minutes **BAKE:** 9 minutes per batch **OVEN:** 375°F **MAKES:** about 60 cookies

1 **cup rolled oats**

½ **cup butter, softened**

1 **cup packed brown sugar**

1 **teaspoon baking soda**

¼ **teaspoon salt**

1 **8-ounce container plain low-fat yogurt**

2 **eggs**

1 **teaspoon vanilla**

2½ **cups all-purpose flour**

1 **cup miniature semisweet chocolate pieces (6 ounces)**

ONE Place oats in a shallow baking pan. Bake in a 375° oven about 10 minutes or until toasted, stirring once. Place toasted oats in a food processor bowl or blender container. Cover and process or blend until ground; set aside.

TWO In a large mixing bowl beat butter with an electric mixer on medium to high speed for 30 seconds. Add brown sugar, baking soda, and salt; beat until combined. Beat in yogurt, eggs, and vanilla until combined. Beat in as much of the flour as you can with the mixer. Using a wooden spoon, stir in the oats and any remaining flour. Stir in chocolate pieces.

THREE Drop dough by rounded teaspoons 2 inches apart on an ungreased cookie sheet. Bake in the 375° oven for 9 to 11 minutes or until bottoms are browned. Transfer to a wire rack to cool.

Nutrition Facts per cookie: 71 cal., 3 g total fat (1 g sat. fat), 12 mg chol., 49 mg sodium, 11 g carbo. (6 g sugar), 0 g fiber, 1 g pro.
Exchanges: ½ Other Carbo., ½ Fat

DOUBLE CHOCOLATE BROWNIES

PREP: 10 minutes **BAKE:** 15 minutes **OVEN:** 350°F **MAKES:** 16 brownies

Nonstick cooking spray

$^1/_4$ **cup butter or margarine**

$^2/_3$ **cup granulated sugar**

$^1/_2$ **cup cold water**

1 **teaspoon vanilla**

1 **cup all-purpose flour**

$^1/_4$ **cup unsweetened cocoa powder**

1 **teaspoon baking powder**

$^1/_4$ **cup miniature semisweet chocolate pieces**

2 **teaspoons sifted powdered sugar (optional)**

ONE Lightly coat the bottom of a 9X9X2-inch baking pan with nonstick cooking spray, being careful not to coat sides of pan.

TWO In a medium saucepan melt butter; remove from heat. Stir in granulated sugar, water, and vanilla. Stir in flour, cocoa powder, and baking powder until combined. Stir in chocolate pieces. Pour batter into prepared pan.

THREE Bake in a 350° oven for 15 to 18 minutes or until a wooden toothpick inserted near the center comes out clean. Cool on a wire rack. Remove from pan. Cut into squares. If desired, sprinkle with powdered sugar.

Nutrition Facts per brownie: 111 cal., 4 g total fat (2 g sat. fat), 8 mg chol., 37 mg sodium, 17 g carbo. (10 g sugar), 0 g fiber, 1 g pro.
Exchanges: 1 Other Carbo., 1 Fat

cut the sugar

Try these Double Chocolate Brownies. They taste great and have $^1/_3$ less sugar than a purchased mix.

let the **kids**

cook!

We all know that kids are more likely to try foods when they've helped make them.
That's why this special section is just for kids! Here you'll find simple recipes for
breakfast foods, sack lunches, and after-school snacks.

Let's Get Cooking

Hey kids! Have you ever wanted to make your own snacks after school? Something different than chips or cookies? How about making your own breakfast or preparing your lunch for school? You can do all these things with this special "kids-only" section and just a little help from an adult.

GETTING STARTED
Ask an adult to help you choose a recipe. Read through the recipe and ask any questions you may have. Have the adult show you how to use the equipment you'll need, especially knives; the stove; and electric appliances, such as the can opener, mixer, blender, and food processor.

STAY CLEAN Before you start to cook, wash your hands. Dry them well and keep them dry so you can get a good grip on your utensils.

Wear an apron to avoid staining your clothes. Roll up loose sleeves and clip hair back from your face. Loose sleeves can drag through food or catch on pan handles; hair in your face can fall in the food (yuck!) or make it hard for you to see.

WATCH FOR SHARP EDGES Pick up a knife by the handle. Always keep the sharp edge pointed away from you and your hand when cutting food. Slice and chop on a cutting board. Leave sharp tools on the counter until you are ready to wash them.

CAREFUL, IT'S HOT! Remember, anything you take from the stove, oven, or microwave oven is hot and will stay hot for a while. Never set a hot pan or dish directly on the counter. Instead place it on a hot pad or wire cooling rack. Use hot pads to handle hot items. If you accidentally touch something hot, immediately hold your hand under cold water.

Tip open lids on saucepans and casserole dishes from the side farthest from you. Turn saucepan and skillet handles to the middle of the stove. This way you won't bump a handle and spill hot food.

KITCHEN TOOL SAFETY Make sure a mixer or blender is turned off before you scrape the sides of the bowl. Unplug the mixer before you put in or take out the beaters.

Don't use electric appliances near water. If an appliance falls into water while it's plugged in, DON'T TOUCH IT. Call an adult for help. Never plug in or unplug an electric appliance while your hands are wet.

Use only microwave-safe equipment in the microwave oven. Foil, foil containers, metal pans, and some glass or pottery dishes can cause sparks.

A Note for Adults
There are no set rules for when a child is ready to handle sharp kitchen tools. Consider the child's desire, dexterity, and ability to focus. When in doubt, start slowly. Children ages 7 to 10 can use a vegetable peeler. Show them how to peel away from the hand holding the food. Children ages 11 and older generally can use a paring knife. Start out with easy-to-slice vegetables that offer little resistance. Kids ages 13 and older can tackle more challenging cutting jobs. Be watchful that increased confidence doesn't breed carelessness.

Keeping Your Food Safe

Just as it's important to keep you safe when cooking, it's also important to keep the food safe. Making your food safe just means keeping the food from getting bacteria on it that would make you sick. To do this, you need to make sure everything is clean as you're cooking, including hands, equipment, and work surfaces. Ask an adult what cleaners you should use. Some cleaners can be dangerous, especially if used the wrong way, so always talk to an adult before using.

It's also important to make sure that the foods you're using in a recipe are clean and okay to use. Here are some helpful tips to follow for tasty and safe foods.

COOK AND EAT ONLY FRESH FOODS. Spoiled foods can smell, look, and taste normal, but even a small bite can make you ill. If in doubt, check the packaging for an expiration date and/or throw it out.

USE A CLEAN PLASTIC CUTTING BOARD. When you cut raw chicken, meat, or fish, do it on a cutting board. Wash the board with hot soapy water after each use and before using with another type of food.

KEEP HOT FOODS HOT. Raw eggs, fish, poultry, and meat must be well-cooked to kill harmful bacteria. Put leftovers into covered containers and refrigerate or freeze them as soon as possible. Remember the two-hour rule: Leftovers should not sit out longer than two hours after a meal.

DON'T EAT RAW EGGS. They may contain harmful bacteria that can make you sick. This also means no raw cookie dough.

USE AN INSTANT-READ THERMOMETER. Poke it into the center of cooked meat before serving to see if it's safely cooked through. Cook ground beef mixtures to 160°F, ground chicken mixtures to 165°F, and chicken breasts to 170°F. Reheat any leftover food to 165°F.

KEEP COLD FOODS COLD. Foods that are typically stored in the refrigerator—hot dogs, for example—should be cold when you touch them. Frozen foods should be icy and firm. Thaw foods overnight in the refrigerator, not on the countertop. Or you can thaw foods in the microwave oven according to the manufacturer's directions if you are going to cook them right away.

DON'T USE CRACKED OR DIRTY EGGS. They may be contaminated with harmful bacteria. After working with eggs, wash your hands, equipment, and the countertop.

WASH FRESH FRUITS AND VEGETABLES. Rinse them well in cool water before eating or preparing them.

UTENSILS

- Cutting board
- Sharp knife
- Toaster
- Table knife

MAKE-IT-FAST WAFFLES

START TO FINISH: 5 minutes **MAKES:** 1 serving

- 1 **frozen waffle**
- ¼ **cup strawberries, 1 small apple, or 1 small banana**
- 1 **tablespoon creamy peanut butter**

ONE Remove the waffle from the package. Let the waffle thaw.

TWO If you are using strawberries, on a cutting board, use a sharp knife to cut the green tops off the strawberries. Throw tops away. Cut the strawberries into slices. If you are using the apple, on the cutting board, use the sharp knife to cut the apple into 4 pieces; cut out the core. Cut the apple into slices. If you are using the banana, remove the peel; throw peel away. On the cutting board, use the knife to cut the banana into slices.

THREE Toast the waffle in the toaster until golden. Use the table knife to spread it with peanut butter. Top with the fruit.

Nutrition Facts per serving: 195 cal., 11 g total fat (2 g sat. fat), 11 mg chol., 342 mg sodium, 19 g carbo. (4 g sugar), 2 g fiber, 6 g pro.
Exchanges: 1 Starch, 1 High-Fat Meat, ½ Fat

get active

Build strength by carrying items like book bags and groceries, instead of putting them in a rolling cart or bag with wheels.

- Toaster
- Measuring spoon
- Small microwave-safe plate
- Microwave oven
- Hot pads
- Fork

HAM WAFFLE-WICH

START TO FINISH: 5 minutes   **MAKES:** 1 serving

1 frozen plain or apple-cinnamon waffle

1 tablespoon sugar-free pancake and waffle syrup product

1 ounce low-fat thinly sliced cooked ham

ONE Remove the waffle from the package. Toast the waffle in the toaster until golden. Drizzle the syrup onto the toasted waffle. Place the ham on the microwave-safe plate. Put ham in microwave oven; close door. Microwave ham on 100% power (high) for 10 seconds. Using hot pads, remove the plate from the microwave oven. Use the fork to put the ham on top of the waffle. Fold in half.

Nutrition Facts per serving: 134 cal., 4 g total fat (1 g sat. fat), 16 mg chol., 606 mg sodium, 17 g carbo. (2 g sugar), 1 g fiber, 8 g pro.
Exchanges: 1 Starch, 1 Lean Meat

get active

Map out a trail with a compass and then walk, jog, bike, or hike the trail.

UTENSILS

- Cutting board
- Sharp knife
- Small bowl
- Measuring spoons
- Small spoon
- Measuring cups
- Serving bowls

EASY BREAKFAST SUNDAES

START TO FINISH: 10 minutes **MAKES:** 2 servings

1 cup blueberries, grapes, strawberries, and/or 2 small bananas

1 8-ounce carton low-fat plain yogurt

1 teaspoon vanilla

Low-calorie sweetener to equal 1 teaspoon sugar

½ to 1 cup ready-to-eat unsweetened cereal, such as round toasted oat cereal, oat square cereal, bran cereal flakes, and/or Grape-Nuts cereal

ONE If you are using strawberries, on the cutting board, use the sharp knife to cut the green tops off the strawberries. Throw tops away. Cut the strawberries into bite-size pieces. If you are using bananas, remove the peel; throw peel away. On the cutting board, use the knife to cut bananas into bite-size pieces.

TWO In the small bowl put yogurt, vanilla, and low-calorie sweetener. Stir with the small spoon until smooth. Divide yogurt mixture in half and spoon each half into one of the serving bowls. Divide cereal and fruit in half and put into bowls with yogurt. Serve right away.

Nutrition Facts per serving: 146 cal., 2 g total fat (1 g sat. fat), 7 mg chol., 150 mg sodium, 24 g carbo. (16 g sugar), 2 g fiber, 7 g pro.
Exchanges: ½ Milk, ½ Fruit, ½ Starch, ½ Fat

let the kids cook!

APPLE PIE OATMEAL

UTENSILS

- Microwave-safe bowl
- Measuring cups
- Hot pads
- Wooden spoon
- Measuring spoons

START TO FINISH: 11 minutes **MAKES:** 1 serving

1 **0.98-ounce envelope plain instant oatmeal**

⅔ **cup water**

¼ **cup unsweetened applesauce**

¼ **teaspoon apple pie spice**

ONE Pour oatmeal into a microwave-safe bowl. Add the water to the oatmeal. Place bowl in microwave oven; close door. Microwave on 100% power (high) for 1 to 2 minutes or until thickened. Use hot pads to remove bowl from the microwave. Stir with a wooden spoon until mixed. Add applesauce and apple pie spice to oatmeal; stir until mixed.

Nutrition Facts per serving: 131 cal., 2 g total fat (0 g sat. fat), 0 mg chol., 84 mg sodium, 25 g carbo. (6 g sugar), 4 g fiber, 4 g pro.
Exchanges: ½ Fruit, 1 Starch, ½ Fat

STOVE TOP DIRECTIONS: Pour ½ cup water into a small saucepan. Place saucepan on a burner; turn on burner to high heat. Heat water to boiling. Turn off burner. Use hot pads to remove saucepan from heat. Place saucepan on wire rack. Pour oatmeal into hot water; stir with a wooden spoon until mixed. Add applesauce and apple pie spice; stir until mixed. Transfer to a bowl.

get active

Gather all the kids in the neighborhood together and play a game of Red Rover.

- Microwave-safe bowl
- Measuring cups
- Hot pads
- Wooden spoon
- Measuring spoons

CINNAMON ROLL OATMEAL

START TO FINISH: 5 minutes **MAKES:** 1 serving

1 .98-ounce envelope plain instant oatmeal

²/₃ cup water

1 tablespoon tub-style light cream cheese

¼ teaspoon ground cinnamon

2 tablespoons raisins (optional)

Low-calorie sweetener (optional)

ONE Pour oatmeal into a microwave-safe bowl. Add the water to the oatmeal. Place bowl in microwave oven; close door. Microwave on 100% power (high) for 1 to 2 minutes or until thickened. Use hot pads to remove bowl from the microwave. Stir with a wooden spoon until mixed. Add cream cheese and cinnamon to oatmeal; stir until mixed. If you like, add raisins or sweeten to taste with low-calorie sweetener.

Nutrition Facts per serving: 134 cal., 4 g total fat (2 g sat. fat), 8 mg chol., 158 mg sodium, 19 g carbo. (1 g sugar), 3 g fiber, 6 g pro.
Exchanges: 1 Starch, 1 Fat

STOVE TOP DIRECTIONS: Pour ½ cup water into a small saucepan. Place saucepan on a burner; turn on burner to high heat. Heat water to boiling. Turn off burner. Use hot pads to remove saucepan from heat. Place saucepan on wire rack. Pour oatmeal into hot water; stir with a wooden spoon until mixed. Add cream cheese and cinnamon to oatmeal; stir until mixed. If you like, add raisins or sweeten to taste with low-calorie sweetener. Transfer oatmeal to a bowl.

UTENSILS

- Glass measuring cup
- 10- to 12-ounce plastic drink bottle with wide top and lid
- Measuring spoons

SUPER SIMPLE
BREAKFAST SHAKE

START TO FINISH: 10 minutes **MAKES:** 1 serving

1 **cup fat-free milk**

2 **teaspoons sugar-free instant chocolate and/or vanilla pudding mix**

1 **to 2 drops vanilla**

Cut-up fresh fruit (optional)

ONE Pour milk into the 10- to 12-ounce plastic drink bottle. Add pudding mix and vanilla. Put the lid on the bottle. Shake bottle until the shake is smooth. Stop shaking and let the bottle set on the counter for 3 to 5 minutes or until the shake thickens a little. If you like, top with cut-up fresh fruit. Drink right away.

Nutrition Facts per serving: 99 cal., 0 g total fat (0 g sat. fat), 5 mg chol., 253 mg sodium, 16 g carbo. (13 g sugar), 0 g fiber, 9 g pro.
Exchanges: 1 Milk

get active

In the fall, rake a huge pile of leaves and then jump in it! See who can rake the biggest pile.

UTENSILS

- Medium saucepan with lid
- Hot pads
- Wire rack
- Colander
- Bowls
- Cutting board
- Sharp knife
- Measuring spoons
- Wooden spoon
- Measuring cup

EGG SALAD
MORNING MIX-UP

PREP: 30 minutes **MAKES:** 4 servings

4 **eggs**

4 **ounces low-fat thinly sliced cooked ham**

2 **tablespoons light mayonnaise or salad dressing**

1 **tablespoon yellow or Dijon-style mustard**

2 **large whole wheat pita bread rounds, 2 whole wheat bagels, or four 6-inch whole wheat tortillas**

ONE Put eggs into the medium saucepan. Add enough cold water to just cover the eggs. Put the saucepan on a burner. Turn the burner to high heat. Heat until the water boils with large bubbles that break quickly. Turn off burner. Using hot pads, remove saucepan from burner. Put saucepan on a wire rack. Put the lid on the saucepan and let stand for 15 minutes. Place the colander in the sink. Drain the eggs and water into the colander. Using hot pads, move eggs from the colander to a bowl filled with ice water. Let the eggs cool completely. Gently tap each egg on the countertop. Roll each egg between the palms of your hands. Peel off eggshell, starting at the large end. Throw away eggshells. On the cutting board, use the sharp knife to cut the eggs in small pieces.

TWO Place the chopped eggs into a bowl. On the cutting board, use the sharp knife to cut ham into small pieces. Add ham, mayonnaise, and mustard to chopped eggs in bowl. Use the wooden spoon to stir egg mixture until mixed.

THREE On the cutting board, use the sharp knife to cut each pita bread round in half. Using your fingers, carefully split each half open (but do not break into 2 pieces) to form a pocket. Spoon 1/3 cup of the egg salad into each pita pocket. Or on the cutting board, use the sharp knife to cut each bagel in half. Top each bagel half with 1/3 cup of egg salad. Or spoon 1/3 cup of egg salad near one edge of each tortilla; roll tortilla around filling.

Nutrition Facts per serving: 231 cal., 10 g total fat (3 g sat. fat), 230 mg chol., 660 mg sodium, 20 g carbo. (1 g sugar), 2 g fiber, 16 g pro.
Exchanges: 1 Starch, 2 Lean Meat, 1/2 Fat

FRUIT AND CHEESE PITAS

START TO FINISH: 20 minutes **MAKES:** 2 servings

2 kiwifruits or ½ cup strawberries

½ cup low-fat cottage cheese

½ cup shredded reduced-fat cheddar cheese (2 ounces)

¼ cup drained pineapple tidbits

1 large pita bread round

2 tablespoons sliced almonds, pecan pieces, or walnut pieces, toasted, if you like (optional)

ONE If you are using kiwi fruits, have an adult remove the peel. On the cutting board, use the sharp knife to cut the kiwi into small pieces. Or if using strawberries, on the cutting board, use the sharp knife to cut the green tops off the strawberries. Throw green tops away. On the cutting board, use the sharp knife to cut the strawberries into small pieces.

TWO Put the kiwi or strawberry pieces, cottage cheese, cheddar cheese, and pineapple tidbits into the small bowl. Use the spoon to stir the mixture together. Set mixture aside.

THREE On the cutting board, use the sharp knife to cut the pita bread round in half. Using your fingers, carefully split each half open (but do not break into 2 pieces) to form a pocket. Use the spoon to put the fruit and cheese mixture into pita halves. If you like, sprinkle with almonds.

Nutrition Facts per serving: 273 cal., 6 g total fat (3 g sat. fat), 22 mg chol., 604 mg sodium, 35 g carbo. (14 g sugar), 4 g fiber, 19 g pro.
Exchanges: 1 Fruit, 1 Starch, 2½ Very Lean Meat, 1 Fat

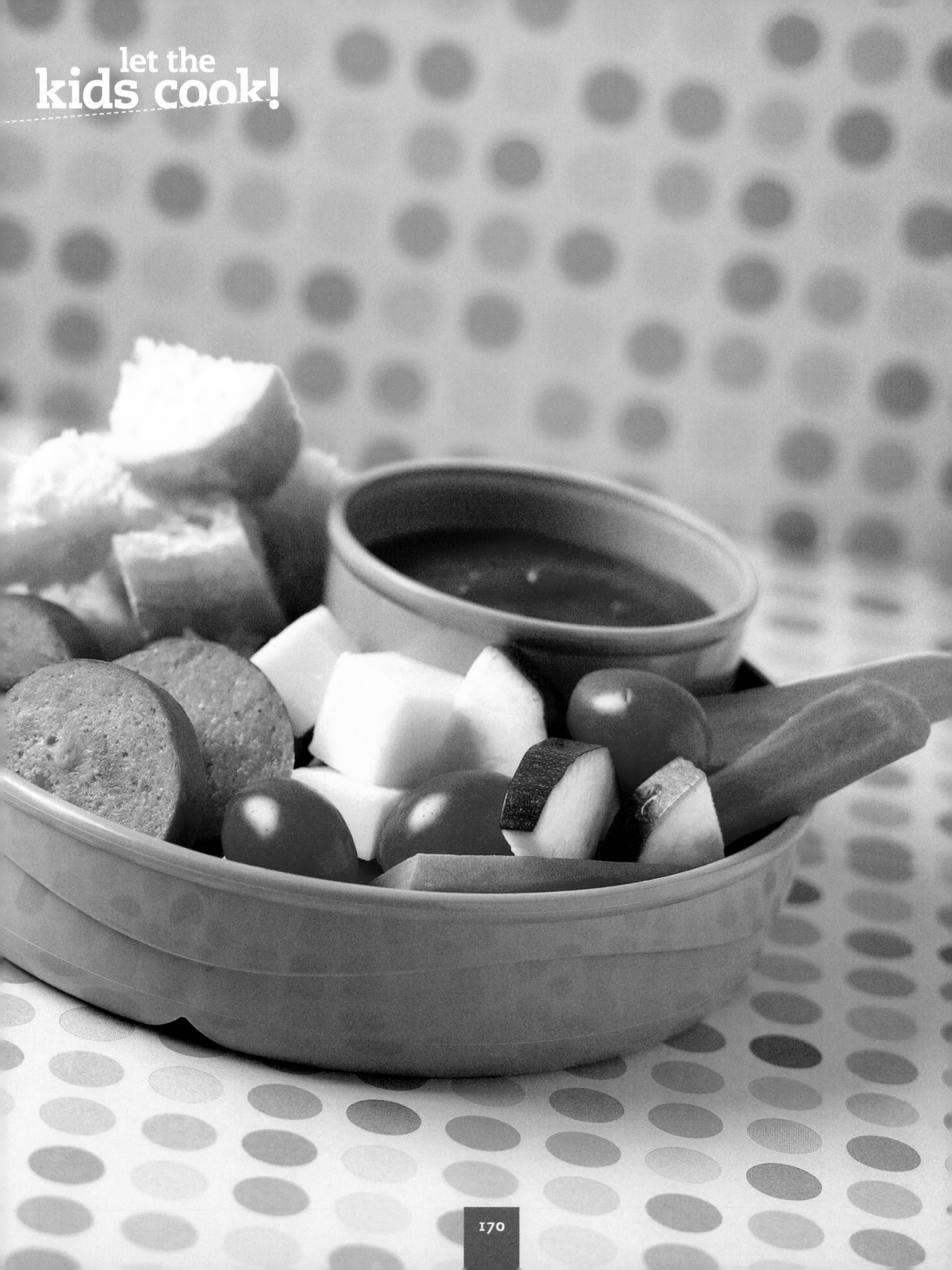

DIP-AND-EAT LUNCH

PREP: 15 minutes **CHILL:** 1 hour **MAKES:** 1 serving

1 ounce smoked turkey sausage

1 ounce mozzarella or provolone cheese

1 ounce Italian bread

½ of a small zucchini, 1 carrot, ½ cup broccoli florets, ½ of a medium green sweet pepper, and/or ½ cup grape or cherry tomatoes

¼ cup tomato sauce

⅛ teaspoon dried Italian seasoning

Dash garlic powder

ONE On the cutting board, use the sharp knife to cut sausage into bite-size slices. On the cutting board, use the sharp knife to cut the cheese into bite-size cubes. On the cutting board, use the sharp knife to cut the bread into bite-size pieces. On the cutting board, use the sharp knife to cut the zucchini, carrot, and/or sweet pepper into bite-size pieces.

TWO Put sausage, cheese, bread, and vegetables into the 2-cup plastic container or the plastic bag. Put the lid on the container or seal the bag; chill for 1 to 6 hours.

THREE Put the tomato sauce, Italian seasoning, and garlic powder in the small container. Stir with a small spoon until combined. Put the lid on the container. Chill container for up to 6 hours. To eat, dip the sausage, cheese, bread, and vegetable pieces in the tomato mixture.

Nutrition Facts per serving: 219 cal., 8 g total fat (4 g sat. fat), 37 mg chol., 957 mg sodium, 22 g carbo. (2 g sugar), 2 g fiber, 15 g pro.
Exchanges: 1 Vegetable, 1 Starch, 2 Lean Meat

let the
kids cook!

UTENSILS

- Cutting board
- Sharp knife
- Measuring cups
- Table knife

SIMPLE SPIRALS

START TO FINISH: 10 minutes **MAKES:** 2 servings

1 small wedge lettuce

1 small tomato

2 7- to 8-inch tomato-basil, spinach, and/or plain flour tortillas

¼ cup light dairy sour cream ranch or chive dip

4 slices very thinly sliced cooked beef, chicken, turkey, or ham (about 2 ounces)

ONE On the cutting board, use the sharp knife to cut the lettuce into small pieces. You should have about ½ cup. On the same cutting board, use the knife to chop the tomato. You should have about ¼ cup. Set the vegetables aside.

TWO Use the table knife to spread each tortilla with 2 tablespoons dip. Place beef on each tortilla. Top with lettuce and tomato. Roll tortilla up tightly. Use the sharp knife to trim off uneven ends and cut each roll into 4 pieces.

Nutrition Facts per serving: 273 cal., 9 g total fat (3 g sat. fat), 34 mg chol., 450 mg sodium, 33 g carbo. (3 g sugar), 1 g fiber, 15 g pro.
Exchanges: ½ Vegetable, 2 Starch, 1½ Lean Meat, 1 Fat

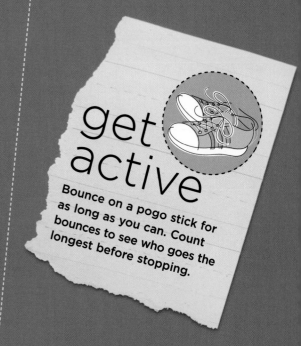

get active

Bounce on a pogo stick for as long as you can. Count bounces to see who goes the longest before stopping.

- Cutting board
- Sharp knife
- Medium bowl
- Measuring cups
- Measuring spoons
- Wooden spoon

RANCH-STYLE TURKEY POCKET

START TO FINISH: 15 minutes **MAKES:** 2 servings

- **1 large whole wheat pita bread round**
- **2 ounces sliced cooked turkey breast**
- **½ of a small tomato**
- **¾ cup packaged shredded broccoli (broccoli slaw mix) or shredded cabbage with carrot (coleslaw mix)**
- **2 tablespoons bottled reduced-calorie ranch salad dressing**

ONE On the cutting board, use the sharp knife to cut the pita bread round in half. Using your fingers, carefully split each half open (but do not break into 2 pieces) to form a pocket. Save pita halves for Step 3.

TWO On the cutting board, use the sharp knife to cut the turkey into bite-size pieces. Place the turkey in the medium bowl. On the cutting board, use the sharp knife to cut the tomato into small pieces. Add tomato pieces to turkey in bowl. Add shredded broccoli and salad dressing to bowl with turkey and tomatoes. Use the wooden spoon to stir the broccoli mixture.

THREE Use the wooden spoon to carefully spoon about half of the broccoli mixture into each pita pocket. Serve right away.

TIP: If packing this for school lunch, prepare as above except do not add salad dressing to the broccoli mixture. Put the salad dressing in a small container with a lid. Put the lid on the container. Stir the dry broccoli mixture with the wooden spoon. Spoon half of the broccoli mixture into each pita pocket. Put the stuffed pitas in self-sealing plastic bags; close the bags. Pack pitas and dressing in an insulated container with a small ice pack for up to 6 hours. Uncover dressing and pour over broccoli mixture in pita pockets.

Nutrition Facts per serving: 174 cal., 5 g total fat (0 g sat. fat), 25 mg chol., 360 mg sodium, 22 g carbo. (1 g sugar), 3 g fiber, 13 g pro.
Exchanges: 1 Vegetable, 1 Starch, 1 Very Lean Meat, 1 Fat

UTENSILS

- Cutting board
- Sharp knife
- Table knife

MINI SUBMARINES

START TO FINISH: 20 min. **MAKES:** 6 servings

3 **6-inch unsliced French-style rolls**

   Yellow mustard

1 **tomato**

6 **ounces thinly sliced cooked ham, roast beef, or turkey**

3 **slices provolone, mozzarella, or Swiss cheese (3 ounces), halved**

3 **lettuce leaves**

ONE On the cutting board, use the sharp knife to carefully make a slit about 4 inches long on the top of each roll. Hollow out a ¾-inch-wide strip of bread along the slit. Use the table knife to spread the inside of each roll with mustard. Set the rolls aside. On the same cutting board, use the sharp knife to cut the tomato into thin wedges.

TWO Divide the ham and cheese evenly among the rolls. Add a lettuce leaf and some of the tomato wedges to each sandwich. Cut the sandwiches in half.

Nutrition Facts per serving: 155 cal., 7 g total fat (3 g sat. fat), 26 mg chol., 641 mg sodium, 12 g carbo. (1 g sugar), 1 g fiber, 10 g pro.
Exchanges: ½ Vegetable, ½ Starch, 1½ Medium-Fat Meat

UTENSILS

- Cutting board
- Sharp knife
- Measuring cups
- 4-cup plastic container with lid or 1-quart self-sealing plastic bag
- Measuring spoons
- Small container with lid

get active

Plan a family treasure hunt. Divide into teams and run, jog, or walk from point to point.

SHAKE-IT-UP
TURKEY SALAD

PREP: 15 minutes **CHILL:** up to 4 hours **MAKES:** 1 serving

¼ of a small cucumber

1 ounce cooked turkey or ham

1 cup packaged mixed salad greens

¼ cup grape or cherry tomatoes

2 tablespoons shredded mozzarella cheese

1 tablespoon sliced almonds or walnut pieces (optional)

2 tablespoons of your favorite bottled reduced-fat or reduced-calorie salad dressing

ONE On the cutting board, use the sharp knife to cut the cucumber into ½-inch pieces (you should have about ¼ cup). On the same cutting board, use the sharp knife to cut the turkey into ½-inch pieces.

TWO In the 4-cup plastic container or 1-quart self-sealing plastic bag, place cucumber, turkey, salad greens, tomatoes, cheese, and, if you like, almonds. Put the lid on the container or seal the bag and chill for up to 4 hours until ready to eat. Place salad dressing in the container; put the lid on the container and chill until ready to eat.

THREE When ready to eat, uncover the salad and dressing; pour dressing over the salad in the container or bag. Put the lid on the container or seal the bag and shake to mix.

Nutrition Facts per serving: 169 cal., 10 g total fat (2 g sat. fat), 41 mg chol., 435 mg sodium, 8 g carbo. (4 g sugar), 1 fiber, 13 g pro.
Exchanges: 1½ Vegetable, 1½ Very Lean Meat, 2 Fat

SHAKE-IT-UP
BLACK BEAN SALAD

UTENSILS

- Can opener
- Measuring cups
- Colander
- Cutting board
- Sharp knife
- 4-cup plastic container with lid or 1-quart self-sealing plastic bag
- Measuring spoons
- Small container with lid

PREP: 15 minutes **CHILL:** up to 6 hours **MAKES:** 1 serving

1 **15-ounce can black beans**

½ **of a small yellow or green sweet pepper**

3 **or 4 purchased baked tortilla chips**

1 **cup packaged mixed salad greens**

¼ **cup grape or cherry tomatoes**

2 **tablespoons shredded reduced-fat cheddar cheese**

2 **tablespoons bottled salsa**

ONE Use the can opener to carefully open the black beans. Measure ¼ cup of the beans (save the rest of the beans for another use). Put the ¼ cup beans in a colander. Rinse beans with cold water and let water drain into the sink. Save beans until Step 3.

TWO On the cutting board, use the sharp knife to cut the sweet pepper into bite-size pieces. Put the pepper pieces in the 4-cup plastic container or 1-quart self-sealing plastic bag. Break tortilla chips into small pieces to equal 2 tablespoons; add them to the peppers in the container or bag.

THREE Add drained black beans, salad greens, tomatoes, and cheese to the pepper and tortilla pieces in the container or bag. Put the lid on the container or seal the bag. Put the salsa in the small container. Put the lid on the container. Eat the salad right away or chill the salad and salsa up to 6 hours.

FOUR When ready to eat, uncover the salad and salsa; pour the salsa over the salad in the container or bag. Put the lid on the container or seal the bag and shake to mix.

Nutrition Facts per serving: 158 cal., 3 g total fat (2 g sat. fat), 10 mg chol., 427 mg sodium, 22 g carbo. (5 g sugar), 7 g fiber, 10 g pro.
Exchanges: 2 Vegetable, 1 Starch, ½ Very Lean Meat

get active

Toss a beach ball and see how long you can keep it in the air. Then try it with a volleyball.

UTENSILS

- 14x12-inch piece of waxed paper
- Measuring cup
- Measuring spoon
- Thin metal spatula

QUICK-AS-A-LICK PRETZEL STICKS

PREP: 10 minutes **MAKES:** 4 servings

¾ **cup reduced-sugar chocolate-flavored puffed corn cereal and/or sweetened fruit-flavored round toasted cereal**

2 **tablespoons creamy peanut butter**

4 **pretzel rods**

ONE Lay the waxed paper on the counter. Spread desired cereal on waxed paper. Set aside. Using the metal spatula, spread peanut butter in a thin layer over half of each pretzel rod. Roll each rod in the cereal so it sticks to the peanut butter. Eat right away or put in an airtight container and store at room temperature for up to 1 day.

Nutrition Facts per serving: 107 cal., 5 g total fat (1 g sat. fat), 0 mg chol., 195 mg sodium, 14 g carbo. (3 g sugar), 1 g fiber, 3 g pro.
Exchanges: 1 Starch, ½ High-Fat Meat

let the kids cook!

get active

On a rainy day, tape your own family workout video of exercise routines to use later.

STICKS AND STONES
TRAIL MIX photo, p. 156-157

START TO FINISH: 5 minutes **MAKES:** 12 servings

2 cups pretzel sticks

1 cup reduced-sugar fruit-flavored round toasted cereal

1 cup reduced-sugar chocolate-flavored puffed corn cereal

1 cup peanuts or sliced almonds

ONE In a large bowl place pretzel sticks, cereals, and peanuts. Stir with the wooden spoon.

Nutrition Facts per serving: 116 cal., 6 g total fat (1 g sat. fat), 0 mg chol., 186 mg sodium, 11 g carbo. (1 g sugar), 1 g fiber, 4 g pro.
Exchanges: 1 Starch, 1 Fat

- Small spoon
- Microwave-safe 6-ounce custard cup or small bowl
- Measuring spoons
- Hot pads

SHORT-CUT APPLE CRISP

START TO FINISH: 10 minutes **MAKES:** 1 serving

1 **4-ounce snack-size container unsweetened applesauce**

⅛ **teaspoon apple pie spice or ground cinnamon**

2 **tablespoons reduced-sugar sugar-coated cornflakes or round toasted multigrain cereal**

1 **tablespoon sliced almonds, pecan pieces, or walnut pieces (optional)**

ONE Uncover applesauce container. Spoon applesauce into a microwave-safe 6-ounce custard cup or small bowl. Use a small spoon to stir in apple pie spice. Place custard cup with applesauce in the microwave. Close door. Microwave, uncovered, on 100% power (high) for 15 to 30 seconds until warm. Use hot pads to carefully remove custard cup from microwave; stir applesauce. Sprinkle cereal over warm applesauce. If you like, sprinkle with nuts. Eat while warm.

STRAWBERRY-APPLE CRISP: Make as directed above except do not add the apple pie spice to the applesauce. Instead, stir 1 teaspoon low-sugar strawberry preserves into the cold applesauce. Heat and serve as directed above in Step 1.

Nutrition Facts per serving: 65 cal., 0 g total fat (0 g sat. fat), 0 mg chol., 25 mg sodium, 17 g carbo. (12 g sugar), 2 g fiber, 0 g pro.
Exchanges: 1 Fruit

UTENSILS

- Sixteen 3-ounce disposable plastic drink cups
- 13×9×2-inch baking pan
- Medium mixing bowls
- Measuring cups
- Wire whisk or rotary beater
- Measuring spoons
- Foil
- Sharp knife
- Wooden sticks

PUDDING LOLLIPOPS

PREP: 25 minutes **STAND:** 15 minutes **FREEZE:** 5 hours **MAKES:** 16 pops

1 4-serving-size package sugar-free instant chocolate or chocolate fudge pudding mix

2 cups fat-free milk

1 4-serving-size package sugar-free instant banana cream, butterscotch, pistachio, vanilla, or white chocolate pudding mix

2 cups fat-free milk

ONE Place sixteen 3-ounce disposable plastic drink cups in a 13×9×2-inch baking pan; set aside.

TWO Put the chocolate pudding mix into a medium mixing bowl. Add 2 cups milk. Use a wire whisk or rotary beater to beat the pudding for 2 minutes or until well mixed. Spoon about 2 tablespoons pudding into each cup. Cover cups with a piece of foil. Freeze for 1 hour.

THREE Place desired flavor pudding mix in another medium bowl. Add 2 cups milk. Use a wire whisk or rotary beater to beat the pudding for 2 minutes or until well mixed. Remove pudding-filled cups from freezer; uncover. Spoon 2 tablespoons of second flavor of pudding over frozen pudding in cups.

FOUR Cover each cup with foil. Make a small hole in center of foil with the sharp knife. Push a wooden stick through the hole and into the top layer of pudding in the cup. Put the baking pan in the freezer. Freeze for 4 to 6 hours or until pudding pops are firm. Remove from freezer. Let stand for 15 to 20 minutes before serving. Remove pudding pops from the cups.

TIP: If you like, switch the order of the pudding in some of the cups. Start with the light-colored pudding and top with the chocolate.

Nutrition Facts per pop: 36 cal., 0 g total fat (0 g sat. fat), 1 mg chol., 194 mg sodium, 7 g carbo. (3 g sugar), 0 g fiber, 2 g pro.
Exchanges: ½ Other Carbo.

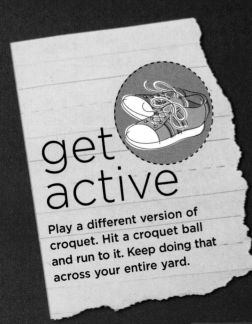

get active

Play a different version of croquet. Hit a croquet ball and run to it. Keep doing that across your entire yard.

Ask your parents to make a copy of this page for each month of the year. You or your parents should write in the month at the top and fill in the days of that month. Then fill in all the things you do each day to keep active.

It can be jumping rope, skipping, running, swimming, playing catch, or anything else that gets your heart and muscles working (so watching TV or playing on the computer would not count!). If you're not sure what to do each day, check out "get active!" boxes throughout this book for ideas.

			MONTH			
SUNDAY	MONDAY	TUESDAY	WEDNESDAY	THURSDAY	FRIDAY	SATURDAY